SUING FOR
PEACE

SUING FOR
PEACE

A Guide for Resolving Life's Conflicts
(without Lawyers, Guns, or Money)

JAMES P. KIMMEL, JR., J.D.

 HAMPTON ROADS
PUBLISHING COMPANY, INC.

The information in this book is not intended to constitute legal advice or to establish an attorney-client relationship between the author and the reader, either directly or indirectly. If you have questions about your legal rights, you are advised to consult a licensed attorney. The intent of this book is to offer information of a general nature to assist people in resolving their conflicts and restoring their happiness. In the event you use the information in this book for yourself, which is your right, the author and publisher assume no responsibility for your actions.

Cover design by Marjoram Productions
Cover illustration "Scales of Justice" © 2005 by Anne L. Louque
"Broken Scales of Justice" concept by James P. Kimmel, Jr., J.D.

Hampton Roads Publishing Company, Inc.
1125 Stoney Ridge Road
Charlottesville, VA 22902

434-296-2772
fax: 434-296-5096
e-mail: hrpc@hrpub.com
www.hrpub.com

If you are unable to order this book from your local
bookseller, you may order directly from the publisher.
Call 1-800-766-8009, toll-free.

Library of Congress Cataloging-in-Publication Data

Kimmel, James P.
  Suing for peace : a guide for resolving life's conflicts / James P. Kimmel, Jr.
     p. cm.
  ISBN 1-57174-452-5 (5-1/2x8-1/2 tp : alk. paper)
  1. Justice--Religious aspects. 2. Forgiveness--Religious aspects. I.
Title.
  BL65.J87K56 2005
  204'.4--dc22
                                   2005001222

ISBN 1-57174-452-5
10 9 8 7 6 5 4 3 2 1
Printed on acid-free paper in Canada

I had learnt the true practice of law. I had learnt to find out the better side of human nature and to enter men's hearts. I realized that the true function of a lawyer was to unite parties riven asunder. The lesson was so indelibly burnt into me that a large part of my time during the twenty years of my practice as a lawyer was occupied in bringing about private compromises of hundreds of cases. I lost nothing thereby—not even money, certainly not my soul.

—Mahatma Gandhi

For Christine,

who practices nonjustice and shows me how.

And for Alexandra and Adam,

who are learning nonjustice,

and showing me how.

Contents

Introduction:
   A Lawyer as Both Legal and Spiritual Advisor? ix

1. *In Pursuit of Justice* 1

2. *Justice Found* 15

3. *The Crisis* 29

4. *The Spiritual Journey* 32

5. *The Awakening* 49

6. *The First Teaching:*
   The Cause of Human Suffering 57

7. *The Second Teaching:*
   The Justice Addiction 67

8. *The Third Teaching:*
   The Most Important Trial of Your Life 75

9. *The Fourth Teaching:* Nonjustice 77

10. *The Fifth Teaching:* The Nonjustice System 84

11. *The Nine Steps of Nonjustice* 93

12. *The Benefits of Practicing Nonjustice* 103

13. *Practicing Nonjustice vs. Preventing Injustice* 106

14. *Practicing Nonjustice vs. Rectifying Injustice* 113

15. *Personal Nonjustice: The* Other *Most
    Important Trial of Your Life* 119

16. *The Nonjustice of Oneness* 123

Appendix: *Questions and Answers about Nonjustice* . .127

A Lawyer as Both Legal and Spiritual Advisor?

It may seem odd for a lawyer, of all people, to be offering do-it-yourself advice for resolving conflicts and achieving peace and happiness. After all, most lawyers depend upon people hiring them to resolve their disputes, and the achievement of peace and happiness is usually considered a spiritual rather than a legal problem. But before you stop reading, you should know that I'm not the first lawyer to step outside his profession and offer direct legal and, yes, *spiritual* guidance in an age of great fear and uncertainty, when traditional means for resolving conflicts have failed and hopes of achieving peace and happiness have dimmed. In fact, the spiritual insights of lawyers at times like these have literally shaped the world in which we live, and chances are you've turned to them often during your life.

Saul of Tarsus, known to most Christians as the Apostle Paul, studied law and was a Jewish prosecutor before his spiritual awakening on the road to Damascus. With the exception of Jesus himself, Paul went on to become the most influential spiritual advisor and revolutionary in the history of Christianity. Likewise, Martin Luther, the leader of the Protestant Reformation and possibly the second greatest Christian revolutionary, studied law before entering monastic life, as did his successor in the reformation, John Calvin. On the darker side of this revolution, St. Thomas More, beheaded under Henry VIII for supporting the Pope, and Michael Servetus, burned at the stake by Calvinists for denying the Divine Trinity, also were lawyers. St. Augustine, St. John of Avila, and St. Francis de Sales all studied law, as did Popes Innocent III, John XXII, Clement VIII, and Benedict XV. William Penn, the Quaker and founder of Pennsylvania, studied law. Mahatma Gandhi, the great Hindu spiritual teacher and revolutionary quoted at the beginning of this book, was a lawyer. So, too, was Muhammad Iqbal, the Muslim philosopher and "Spiritual Father of Pakistan." Among noted writers, poets, and musicians who can be said to have brought spiritual insight to their fields, Leo Tolstoy, Franz Kafka, John Donne, George Frideric Handel, and (some say) William Shakespeare all studied law.

Why so many lawyers at the center of spiritual change? Possibly because law and religion are concerned with many of the same things: justice, happiness, the resolution of disputes, the discernment of fairness, the imposition of judgment, and the punishment and redemption of wrongdoers.

The skills necessary for becoming a successful lawyer (education, concentration, logical thinking, and persuasive writing and speaking) also happen to be useful for becoming a successful spiritual revolutionary.

Of course, not all lawyers go on to become spiritual revolutionaries, and not all spiritual revolutionaries are lawyers. Spiritual revolutionaries tend to have life experiences different from most of us. First, they often witness or endure a particular form of human suffering universal to all mankind rather than confined to an isolated event. Second, in attempting to relieve this suffering, they come to identify its underlying cause as a conflict between a spiritual truth of great importance and the institutions and beliefs of the world around them. Third, after unsuccessfully attempting to avoid and reason their way out of this conflict, they embark upon a spiritual journey to resolve it. Fourth, this spiritual journey transforms them, giving them new insight into the nature of reality, and new power to reshape the world to fit this vision—even if it means confronting authority and challenging established ways of thinking.

The book in your hands chronicles such a conflict in our time, and the transforming spiritual journey that resolved it and promises to reshape our world. The conflict at stake here, and its resolution, are of the utmost importance to all people in this age of terroristic threats and easy violence: it is the conflict between the pursuit of *justice* and the pursuit of *happiness*. For at the root of every terroristic threat and every deliberate act of violence lies a misguided attempt to find happiness by pursuing justice.

Let me explain.

Although I had dedicated my life as a lawyer to the pursuit of justice, something very strange and unexpected happened during my legal career. I began to see that the more justice I won for my clients and myself, the less happy my clients and I became. I'm speaking here of "justice" as it has come to be used most often in our society: as a polite, politically correct synonym for punishment, payback, revenge, retribution, and vengeance—in other words, the justice we seek most often when we file lawsuits, imprison criminals, kidnap hostages, wage wars, and engage in personal acts of retaliation. This type of justice stands in stark contrast to the justice less often associated with fundamental fairness and equity *without winners or losers.* To make the distinction between forms of justice more clear, here's a quick economic and statistical snapshot of the type of justice I'm talking about.

According to the United States Bureau of Justice Statistics, in the year 2001, the United States spent $167 billion on *criminal justice* (that's police, prisons, and courts). At the state and local level, this roughly equates to the total amount of money spent on health care and hospitals (*New York Times,* May 3, 2004). Our criminal justice system in 2001 employed 2.3 million people, incarcerated 2.1 million people, executed sixty-six people, and processed more than 14 million criminal cases through the courts. Add to this *military justice* spending of $306 billion (the cost for our armed forces to pursue justice on an international scale, such as the recent wars in Afghanistan and Iraq), with 1.4 million active duty soldiers and 1.2 million reserves, and the combined price tag of pursuing criminal and military justice in the United States for the year 2001 alone was approximately $473 billion, with 4.9 million people employed in the process (Congressional Budget Office, January 26, 2004; Department of Defense, January 28, 2001).

On the *civil justice* side of the ledger, 22 million civil lawsuits were filed in federal and state courts in 2001 (Bureau of Justice Statistics, 2004; National Center for State Courts, 2002). There's no precise way of calculating the cost of all these lawsuits, but we do know that total revenue for the legal services industry as a whole that year was $175 billion (this would include nonlitigation activities, such as contract drafting, but wouldn't include the costs of increased insurance premiums and lost productivity caused by engaging in civil litigation) (U.S. Census Bureau, January 15, 2003). We also know that approximately 650,000 lawyers were employed in the United States in 2001—compared to only 583,000 physicians and surgeons and just 36,450 religious clergy (U.S. Bureau of Labor Statistics, 2004). *That brings the total annual cost of pursuing justice in the United States to approximately $648 billion, employing more than 5.6 million people who imprisoned 2.1 million people and prosecuted 36 million court cases, two wars, and countless other police and military actions.* And none of this includes the innumerable unreported personal acts of justice we engage in every day, like taking revenge against friends, family, co-workers, and others who wrong us in ways both large and small.

The picture I want you to see here is that, as a society, we consider the pursuit of justice one of our most important goals and, accordingly, devote vast amounts of our resources to it—more than half a trillion dollars. All of which makes rather shocking—if not preposterous—my unexpected discovery as a lawyer that the more justice we win, the less happy we seem to be. Could it really be that the very thing we want most as a people is the very thing that's making us miserable?

I thought at first I was surely misperceiving the situation.

Even as a young child, I understood that we pursue justice to secure our happiness and, most importantly, to restore it when it has been taken from us. Indeed, this is exactly why I'd become a lawyer—to learn how to acquire and use justice to protect my own happiness and the happiness of my family and friends. But the strange thing was that from my earliest days as a criminal prosecutor and as a law clerk to a federal judge, to my years of practice as a civil lawyer for both the very wealthy and the very poor, I began to notice that every time I won justice for my clients, the sudden burst of pleasure and exhilaration we experienced was followed by a big letdown in which we were left somehow feeling worse but wanting more. I started noticing this in my personal life as well. When I pursued justice against anybody— my wife, family, friends, business associates, or simply people rude to me in traffic—I experienced an immediate surge of gratification followed by a much longer period of unhappiness. Conversely, if I didn't pursue justice against these people, my life seemed more peaceful, content, and happy. Then I began witnessing this phenomenon all around me—in stores and restaurants, at sporting events, within organizations, between communities, throughout the entire world. Everywhere I turned, I saw that each attempt to pursue justice by a wronged person, group, or nation succeeded only in producing more conflict, suffering, and unhappiness. On the other hand, each time justice wasn't pursued, peace and happiness seemed to be restored more quickly and abundantly for everyone, including those who'd been wronged and those who'd wronged them.

These observations created a crisis in my life that placed my identity as a lawyer at odds with my spiritual self. I'd always believed God not only pursues justice against us when we sin but wants us to pursue justice against those who harm us, as a way of teaching them a lesson. Many religions are based upon this understanding and preach it with great conviction. Yet I found my spiritual self drawn increasingly toward the teachings of Jesus and other masters who counsel forgiveness as the path to happiness and the only sane response to wrongdoing. How could these two seemingly contradictory spiritual teachings—pursuing justice versus offering forgiveness—be reconciled? And was this conflict between teachings also the source of the conflict between justice and happiness I was experiencing as a lawyer and within the world around me? Might justice be a variable in some mind-boggling Einstein-like equation of opposites, like $J = IU^2$, where J = Justice, I = Injustice and U = Unhappiness? In short, was the legal profession to which I'd devoted my life, and which offers justice as its greatest gift to society, delivering humanity from suffering or enslaving us?

I found no easy answers to these questions. As my dilemma intensified, it began taking a toll on my personal life and what had been a very successful legal career. I initially attributed my distress to the pressures of practicing law, eventually reducing my legal practice to part-time and then nearly ending it altogether. But still I found no relief. I considered other occupations, including becoming an Episcopal priest, but none of these possibilities stilled my soul or held out the promise of resolving the conflict that tormented me. Like any lawyer, I tried to argue and reason my way out of this crisis, but I was eventually forced to accept the fact that the problem wasn't my career choice. My misery was caused by an irreconcilable conflict between the pursuit of justice in our world and the pursuit of happiness in our souls. I would find no peace until this conflict was resolved.

With nowhere else to turn, and with very little left to lose, I embarked upon what became a spiritual journey lasting fifteen years. During this journey, I studied the justice teachings of the world's seven great religions and came to the puzzling conclusion that two of them theologically embrace the pursuit of justice, three reject it, and two are somewhat equivocal. With no unanimity among organized religions, I dove deeper into the spiritual world itself, praying, meditating, and reading the great religious and literary texts of the ages that have wrestled with these questions. Unfortunately, I found no decisive answers there either, and became so desperate I turned to writing novels in an attempt to play out the conflict at a safe distance. This brought me temporary relief, but when I was able to resolve the conflict on paper for my characters and not in my own life, I broke down in despair.

It was at this point, when I'd given up searching for answers and surrendered completely to the paradox and my inability to solve it, that I experienced a sudden spiritual awakening that offered me startling new clarity and insight into the complex relationship between justice and happiness. Over time, I was able to distill this insight into five distinct teachings about the nature of human suffering, conflicts, justice, forgiveness, and peace. These teachings not only resolved the crisis in my own life and became a powerful tool in my legal practice, but they are of such singular importance and universal truth that I believe they hold out the promise of ending much of the suffering and anguish in our world. That may sound like a tall promise, but if you read on, I'm sure you'll find cause here for much celebration and joy. With this book, I want to share with you the lessons from my lifelong pursuit of justice, my spiritual journey to reconcile justice with happiness, and the five teachings that can resolve any conflict and bring immediate peace and happiness into *your* life.

What are these teachings?

Well, unlike what you've probably been taught most of your life, you're about to discover that the pursuit of justice is the primary *cause* of human suffering, not the antidote. This becomes obvious when you think about it. We live in a world in which schoolchildren kill each other to get justice, adults engage in every form of malice in the name of justice, terrorists indiscriminately massacre thousands of people under the delusions of justice, and nations go to war waving the blood-red flag of justice. *All* hurtful acts are, at their root, motivated by the pursuit of justice. Hence, the First Teaching is that the pursuit of justice itself is the primary cause of human-inflicted suffering in our world.

The Second Teaching is that despite the suffering we inflict upon ourselves by pursuing justice, we continue to crave it anyway because we're literally *addicted* to it and see no viable alternative. Science is now revealing to us that, like a narcotic, the pursuit of justice stimulates the gratification and pleasure centers in our brains, leaving us feeling great at first but then feeling worse and wanting more. Like a narcotics pusher, the justice system promises us happiness but produces suffering. The only alternative to pursuing justice—forgiveness—seems impossible when our happiness has been taken away and we're in so much pain.

The Third Teaching follows from the first two: *The most important trial in your life each day is the trial of the people who wrong you.* During this trial, you're asked to choose between getting justice and experiencing happiness. If you choose to seek justice against your enemies, you cause yourself to suffer. If you choose not to seek justice against your enemies, you end your suffering and restore your happiness. Thus, it's *your* freedom that's at stake during this trial, not your enemy's. The outcome of this trial will determine your health, happiness, and peace of mind; it will affect your relationships, family, job, nation, and world.

The Fourth Teaching contains the secret to winning the most important trial of your life, breaking the justice addiction, and restoring your happiness. In the sacred space between Gandhi's teaching of nonviolence—which targets the worst symptoms of pursuing justice—and Jesus' teaching of unconditional forgiveness—which we find so difficult to achieve—lies a previously unrecognized Middle Step. This Middle Step is called *nonjustice,* meaning "to abstain from the pursuit of justice." The teaching of nonjustice holds that even when we're unable to forgive our enemies, we can break the justice addiction and restore our happiness by taking the less difficult Middle Step of abstaining from the pursuit of justice and not further harming *ourselves.* By practicing nonjustice, we end the cycle of self-inflicted suffering and convert the affirmative act of forgiveness from theoretical possibility into spiritual certainty.

The Fifth Teaching offers us a reliable step-by-step method for practicing nonjustice. In the sacred space between our secular justice systems and our rich religious traditions lies *The Nonjustice System.* Combining jurisprudence with spirituality, The Nonjustice System contains nine simple but powerful steps for practicing nonjustice and winning the most important trial of your life *without lawyers, judges, or the justice system.* Following these nine steps, you are taught how to sue your enemies for peace and are led gently to the inevitable conclusion that you win the most important trial of your life not when the guilty verdict is rendered and the sentence is imposed but when nonjustice is practiced and the pursuit of justice is ended.

While only time can tell the extent of the spiritual and legal revolution these teachings might hasten, there's no doubt that those who abide by them will experience a personal revolution. When Martin Luther nailed his Ninety-Five Theses to the door of Wittenberg Church in 1517, he had no idea he was launching the Protestant Reformation. This book represents a Ninety-Five Theses for our time, nailed to the courthouse door. I'm nailing it there because the modern justice system has become, in loosely analogous ways, like the Christian Church in the sixteenth century, trafficking in paid indulgences to resolve disputes but producing only suffering and unhappiness in the process. Just as Luther argued that we need not pay a priest or pope to obtain relief from our sins against God, one of the teachings in this book is that we need not pay a lawyer or judge to obtain relief from our grievances against each other. In fact, doing so often makes matters worse.

This isn't legal advice you've heard before—certainly not from a lawyer. Yet when Mahatma Gandhi transformed himself from a lawyer into a religious teacher, he observed that his regard for jurisprudence actually increased because he "discovered in it religion." He also observed that "to see the universal and all-pervading Spirit of Truth face to face one must be able to love the meanest of creation as oneself." The teachings in this book unite jurisprudence with spirituality to make seeing the Spirit of Truth face to face possible for all of us.

SUING FOR
PEACE

ONE

In Pursuit of Justice

My love affair with justice began when I was a child. My earliest recollection of its bittersweet taste is the day my younger brother wrestled my toy truck from me and I bunched up my fist and punched him for it.

Justice swift and justice sure.

I was minding my own business, playing happily with my truck, when my brother snatched it from my hands and with it my happiness. By taking his happiness from him (by punching him), I believed my happiness would come back to me. This is the root logic of all acts of justice, from brothers fighting over trucks to nations going to war.

Like warfare, however, my simple act of justice triggered a chain of events not so easily foreseen—at least not by a young child. My brother cried. My mother slapped me for

1

punching him and making him cry. I cried. I slammed the truck on my brother's foot because he'd caused my mother to slap me and make me cry. My brother cried some more. My mother told me to go to my room. I told my mother I hated her. My mother cried because she'd slapped me and sent me to my room and now I hated her. I cried in my room because none of this was fair. And my father . . . well, he never cried. He only got involved when my mother couldn't make us cry.

Rather than dissuade me or my family from pursuing justice again, this chain of events, and hundreds more like it, actually strengthened our resolve to find it. Justice became our quest. We believed the last person to get justice was always the person who was right, and this made the last person to get justice the winner. The prize for winning was the restoration of happiness—a return to the state we were in before we were wronged.

My parents were great lovers of justice. If my brother or I did something to disturb their happiness, my parents made sure we paid the consequences. This was a given, and so we avoided doing too many things wrong. Between parents and children, parents are almost always the last to get justice, and so they're almost always the winners.

My parents brought their passion for justice into their marriage as well. If my father did something that upset my mother (which was often), then she had the right to make him miserable to regain her happiness. If my mother did something to upset my father (also often), then he had the right to make her miserable to regain his happiness. My parents exercised these rights they'd accumulated all the way through three separations, horrific fights, clinical depression, the occasional minor violence, two terrorized children, several affairs and, finally, mercifully, a divorce. They were locked in a battle to see who'd be the last one to get justice and win. This battle lasted eighteen years. At the end of it, each claimed victory and went off in separate directions, bitter and emotionally crippled, still searching for that one final act of justice that would restore their happiness.

Now, all this may sound insane, but in fact it's the way most people and nations operate. The American Declaration of Independence lists the pursuit of happiness as one of our three inalienable rights as human beings; but when our happiness is taken, the pursuit of justice stands ready to take it back. The Revolutionary War between the American colonists and the British colonialists was, in the minds of both sides, a "just war"—meaning a war in the pursuit of justice rather than a war of conquest. The British believed the Americans were interfering with their right to happily rule the colonies they had created, and the Americans believed the British were interfering with their right to happily rule the country they had created. This gave rise to the right of both parties to pursue justice against each other. Like my parents' marriage, many battles were fought during the Revolutionary War and much suffering was endured. In the end, we Americans appeared to be the last to get justice and win, thereby restoring our happiness. But like my parents, we were bitter and emotionally crippled for many years—so much so that we tried two different forms of government and waged a bloody civil war amongst ourselves that left more than 600,000 Americans dead. Even today, we're still a nation searching for that one final act of justice that will restore our national happiness. The pursuit of justice has been duly sealed with blood, sweat, and tears into our laws, legal systems, and psyches as our fourth inalienable right. The Pledge of Allegiance, repeated by American school children every morning, ends by declaring that we are "one nation, under God, indivisible, with liberty and justice for all."

My relationship with God as a child was grounded firmly in principles of justice. My paternal grandfather was an evangelical Christian minister in the tobacco-growing country of southern Virginia. He was a simple but powerful preacher, earnest and energetic, widely admired and loved by his congregations, and especially so by his grandchildren. He was playful, funny, and kind, but he could be deadly serious too. He preached the message that God is justice, pure and simple. It went something like this: "We're sinners, all of us; we've done things to upset God's happiness. Therefore, God's gonna pursue justice against us by sending us to hell to take away our happiness. We can avoid this by accepting Jesus as our Savior because God got His happiness back by taking Jesus' happiness and crucifying him. But you've got to accept Jesus as your Savior to get this kind of deal. If you don't, then you're for sure goin' to hell because God's happy when we accept Jesus and He's unhappy when we don't. God gets his happiness back by taking our happiness away . . . for all eternity."

Although my grandfather was an evangelical Christian, his daughter-in-law, my mother, was a moderate Episcopalian and insisted her children be raised that way. The Episcopal Church has considerably more nuance and liturgy than my grandfather did, but its core message is basically the same: accept Jesus and be saved; don't accept Jesus and, well . . . let's just say unpleasant things will happen and leave it at that. Such is the law of Divine Justice.

I had no problem whatsoever accepting Jesus, so I knew I was on the right side of this equation and all was well for my soul. In fact, I loved Jesus (and still do). If God was an angry parent seeking justice, then Jesus was my mischievous brother, slipping me between God's legs and through the door of heaven before I got swatted. Who wouldn't want a brother like that? This took care of my eternity, but it didn't do anything about my today. I still had a life to live and my happiness to protect. Jesus wasn't around anymore, so it was up to me.

The problem became acute early on. Throughout my childhood, my father liked to go out drinking several nights a week. He'd come home late and inebriated. This upset my mother and terrified me. I loved my father desperately. I was afraid he'd be killed in a car accident. So my deal with God was this: If I stay awake and keep praying to You, You bring my dad home safely to me. Justice, pure and simple. If I didn't keep up my end of the bargain and pray, then I'd suffer the consequences and my dad (my happiness) would be taken from me.

I prayed and lay awake a lot as a child. I went to bed around nine or ten, but my father usually didn't come home before midnight, and often not until 2 A.M. I started off the night praying for his safe return and then adding prayers for the welfare of others. I figured if I could keep my dad alive, I should be able to keep them alive too. So there I was, this little boy in his bed, single-handedly saving the people he cared about from calamity. All my relatives, friends, and pets were covered, and this made me feel good. As the hours dragged on, and with all these preliminaries out of the way, I prayed about anything else I could think of. I had long serious talks with God about the world and how it works, and long rambling silly talks about the world and how it works. We had great conversations, God and I.

Sometimes my dad would surprise me and come home before midnight. These were good nights. I'd whisper "thank you" to God and roll over and go to sleep. Other times, my dad would push it. These were bad nights. When two o'clock rolled around and he still wasn't home, my praying intensified, and then it was all about my dad. I imagined what it would be like if he were killed. I rehearsed everything—getting the news, being hysterical, going to his funeral, seeing his coffin disappear into the earth. The terror of this helped keep me awake and praying. If 2:30 came and he still wasn't home, I panicked. By this point, I was convinced he'd been in an accident and started listening for the telephone to ring. I became angry with God for allowing it to happen—but not too angry in case there was still hope.

Fortunately for me, there was always hope. I learned that God's justice was certain, and my happiness was guaranteed as a result. God never broke his promise if I never broke mine. Eventually, rarely past three, I'd hear the crunch of the gravel and my father's car pulling into the driveway. I'd whisper "thank you" to God and roll over and go to sleep, my work done for the night.

During the daytime, I found myself pursuing justice with the same determination. When I was twelve years old, my parents purchased my great-grandfather's farm in central Pennsylvania and we moved there to live. My great-grandfather was an insurance agent, but he liked owning a farm and kept a small herd of black angus cows and some chickens. My father was also an insurance agent. He had no intention of farming the land, but he liked the idea of living in the country. I liked it too.

Unlike me, most of the boys around our place lived on working dairy farms. They and their parents rose before sunrise each day to milk and feed their cows and do their chores. This fascinated me, and I wanted to be their friend and spend time on their farms. But even though my great-grandfather and I continued to raise cows and chickens on our farm, the *real* farm boys didn't like it that we weren't *real* farmers. In fact, they seemed to resent it very much. These boys were bigger than me. There were many of them, and I was on their turf. So they exercised these advantages every chance they got, taunting, bullying, and picking on me from the time I stepped onto the school bus in the morning until the time I stepped off in the afternoon. This went on for five years.

I tried to earn their friendship and respect. I enrolled in the vocational agriculture program at my school and learned how to care for animals, raise crops, and repair farm equipment. I joined the Future Farmers of America. I went to farm shows and rodeos. I raised hogs. And I came to enjoy farming very much. I thought I'd really like to be a farmer someday. I loved being outdoors, handling animals, and driving the big tractors and combines. But the more I tried to be like the farm boys, the more they resented me. Since I was in most of their classes at school, they had many opportunities to pick on me, and they never let one pass. Over time, they came to despise me on sight, and I came to despise them. Oh, how I despised them.

The farm boys had rejected me completely, and I wanted justice. Since there were more of them and they were bigger, my only recourse was to spite them all by leaving them behind in the vocational agriculture program, joining the academic program, and participating in sports. The farm boys hated the academic and athletic kids even more than they hated a half-farmer like me.

Like most of the farm boys, I'd been a poor student up to that point, so my chances of achieving academic success were slim. But justice is a powerful motivator. Within a year, I went from getting mostly C's and D's on my report cards with dreams of being a farmer to getting mostly A's and dreams of going to college. College for me was still quite a reach, however. Nobody on either side of my family had earned a college diploma, and of the two hundred kids who graduated from my rural high school each year, no more than ten or twenty made it. Nevertheless, the possibility was there, and I was suddenly being looked upon by my teachers and classmates as one of the brighter kids in school. In addition, despite my lack of athletic ability, I performed reasonably well in track and field and had begun making friends among the athletic elite of the school, who'd previously ignored me as one of the farm boys. All in all, it was a rather remarkable transformation.

These changes in my social status within the school had the desired effect upon the farm boys. I'd separated myself from them academically, athletically, and socially, succeeding despite their best attempts to stop me. Now it was *me* who was shunning them, and the justice of this was tasting oh, so sweet. Unfortunately, like the time my brother took my truck and I punched him for it, this sweet flow of justice triggered a chain of events I hadn't predicted. Since I was getting even with the farm boys, they wanted justice themselves, and the only way they could do this was by escalating the violence against me. Instead of calling me names, tripping me in the hallways, and pushing me into lockers, they started punching and kicking me whenever they saw me. I led a miserable existence outside the classroom, but I wasn't about to tell my teachers what was happening. They couldn't protect me, and the attacks would only increase. More importantly, each time the farm boys attacked, I knew I was getting justice. I was willing to suffer because I knew they were suffering as well.

But my stubbornness only increased the stakes.

When the farm boys earned their drivers' licenses, they turned to assaulting not only me but our house. It started with smashing and blowing up our mail box in the middle of the night. When that wasn't enough, they threw rotten eggs from their farms all over the front of our house. When that wasn't enough, they threw rocks and broke a few windows. My father called the state police, but the officer said they couldn't do much without a witness and "it was all just pranks" anyway. So the attacks continued. The farm boys not only threw rotten eggs against the house, but they broke into my father's car at night and smashed rotten eggs all over the inside of it.

And then came the final straw.

Late one night, we heard suspicious engine noises, as if they were launching another attack. We switched on the floodlights and looked out the windows but didn't see anything and went back to bed. In the morning, one of my jobs before going to school was to feed and water the cows and make sure our beagle, Polly, had food and water. When I went to Polly's pen, I found her lying in a pool of blood with a bullet hole in her head.

There's no point trying to explain how I felt. There aren't words for it.

A few nights later, the farm boys came back and blew up our mailbox again, but this time I was waiting and my parents weren't home. I should mention that game hunting is very popular in this part of Pennsylvania. I'd been shooting guns since I was eight years old, and I was given a shotgun for my twelfth birthday—my first year of eligibility for a hunting license. We maintained a small arsenal of weapons in our house for this purpose, and among them my father had a .32 caliber revolver. When the mailbox blew up, I grabbed the revolver from his nightstand and ran out the door after the farm boys.

Down the narrow country road I raced in my mother's car, reaching speeds over one hundred miles per hour, cursing and swearing at the top of my lungs, tears streaming down my face. I'd had enough, and now it was time to make them pay. It was time for me to get the final act of justice and declare myself the winner.

I caught up to their trucks quickly and chased them into one of their farms. They roared down the lane to the barn and jumped out. I followed and skidded to a stop behind them. During all these years of abuse, I'd never confronted them and they seemed stunned. They just stood there in the headlights, like whitetail deer in the middle of the road, waiting to see what I'd do. The gun rested on the passenger seat. I put my hand on it and with the other hand reached for the door.

But then I stopped.

Maybe with all those long nights of praying, God

thought he owed me a favor. Whatever the reason, I suddenly saw very clearly that I wouldn't be the last one to get justice. Even if I killed them all, they'd win posthumously. I'd go to jail and everything I'd worked for in school would be wasted. I'd be hurting myself as much or more than I'd be hurting them. It just wasn't worth it. I took my hand off the gun, backed down the lane, and drove home.

"Thank you, God," I whispered.

The farm boys never knew I had a gun with me in the car that night, but for some reason they never bothered me or our house again.

With these experiences behind me, I came to regard religion and justice as two sides of the same coin. Contemplating my future in high school, I gave much consideration to becoming an Episcopal priest. I admired my grandfather, the fundamentalist preacher. He was spreading the news about eternal justice and bringing people to eternal happiness. I'd been an acolyte in my church, and I loved the mystery and pageantry of the Eucharist. I liked public speaking and learned I was good at it. I'd found a part-time job at the local radio station as a disc jockey, news anchor, and reporter. I became the public address system announcer at my high school and the president of an important student service organization. I was asked to deliver the Memorial Day address to our small town and ride in the parade. I was even asked by the rector of my church to give a sermon during my senior year, on the Day of Pentecost, which is the day Christians believe the Holy Spirit descended upon Jesus' disciples and gave them the power to preach in different tongues. Yes, becoming an Episcopal priest seemed like a good fit for me; it might have been my divine destiny. But I just couldn't bring myself to do it. Priests seemed concerned with justice and happiness only after we were dead; but, as I said earlier, I wasn't worried about the afterlife. I believed Jesus would take care of all that. I was more concerned about justice and happiness *in this life.*

Having lived a difficult childhood for what I believed was a lack of justice, having seen my parents tear each other apart for the same reason, and having nearly committed murder because of it, I *craved* justice by the time I graduated from high school. I was convinced that what awaited me in the world was more suffering and unhappiness. The news media screamed it day after day. People were constantly being hurt and wronged by other people. It really was survival of the fittest out there. If I wanted to protect myself and my happiness, I knew I'd need to arm myself to the teeth with justice. I'd need to learn how to find justice, how to use it when I found it, and how to make more of it. I'd need to learn justice's secrets, because I was determined to never again be without its comforts—and to never again suffer as I'd suffered during the first eighteen years of my life.

But how could I become an expert in the art of justice? I looked around and realized that, in this life, as opposed to the afterlife, lawyers are the true priests and judges the true prophets, delivering justice to the masses. Lawyers and judges are the keepers of the spirit and of the liturgy of justice. They officiate at the great temples where justice is practiced and perform its most sacred rites and rituals. They declare what is just and unjust and who is just and unjust. They wield the authority to bless and to condemn. They select whom to spare and whom to punish. They exercise the power to give and take property, liberty, happiness, and life itself. No cleric—not a pope, chief rabbi, jagadguru, mullah, lama, Zen master, or bodhisattva—possesses such vast jurisdiction and power in this lifetime.

The more I studied it, the more I came to realize that the pursuit of justice has become, in both practice and effect, the greatest religion of our society. In times of grief, want, anger, and despair, and also in times of great fortune and abundance, we may turn inwardly to God, but only for a moment. God doesn't give us money judgments when we've been injured or our loved ones have been killed. God doesn't prosecute criminals and put them in jail. God doesn't resolve contract disputes, set alimony payments, foreclose on mortgages, evict tenants, sue employers, contest wills, bankrupt companies, or enforce civil rights, antitrust, environmental, property, or securities laws. God doesn't legislate; nor does God bureaucratize. God doesn't operate police departments, intelligence agencies, or prisons. God doesn't command armies, fly fighter planes, or sail battle ships. God doesn't make war. Nor, when times are good, does God advise us how to protect our treasures of money, property, and fame. You won't find God in court defending the innocent and the oppressed from those who would try to take their possessions, freedom, or lives. Nor will you find God writing birth certificates, marriage certificates, or death certificates. From the cradle to the grave, all these things are within the province of justice and its high priests and prophets. For most of us, whether the chips are up or down, it's more often "in justice we trust" than in God. The Religion of Justice has become the greatest religion of our society because it claims virtually all of us as followers—

both believers and nonbelievers alike. It's exempt from the constitutional prohibition against state-sponsored religion because it's synonymous with the state itself.

With all the advantages justice has to offer in this lifetime, making a career choice became very easy for me. I was convinced, deep down in my heart, that I'd been called from an early age to preach the gospel of justice and to join its priesthood. I wanted it more than anything else in the world. I was prepared to dedicate my life to it, and I knew I'd be good at it.

I would become a lawyer.

Two

Justice Found

Something unusual happened to me during law school. I found justice, all right, and I learned how to use it and how to make more of it. But once I had it, I wasn't so sure I wanted it after all.

During my final year at the University of Pennsylvania Law School, I completed an internship at the Philadelphia District Attorney's Office. As a certified intern, I was allowed to try misdemeanor cases in the municipal court and conduct felony preliminary hearings in the district court. These cases ranged from shoplifting and narcotics possession to burglary, robbery, and aggravated assault with a deadly weapon. Just about the only cases off limits to me as an intern were rape and murder. I was assigned to work with an assistant district attorney who had sixty cases to try each day.

She would give me twenty of her cases to prepare and try on my own. I spent my afternoons and evenings after class calling and subpoenaing victims, witnesses, and police officers. The next morning, I'd search for them in the crowded courtroom, hurriedly go over their testimony and then wait for my cases to be called.

Of the twenty cases assigned to me each week, usually no more than three would actually be tried. The others were either continued because the defendant failed to appear (in which event my job was to convince the judge to issue a bench warrant for his or her arrest), continued because the victim or a witness failed to appear (in which event my job was to convince the judge not to dismiss the case), or resolved without a trial because I was able to negotiate a guilty plea with the public defender. I prayed all of them would go away like this. I was scared to death to try cases. My entire body trembled in the courtroom, and I used the bathroom a lot.

Keep in mind that I'd been raised on a farm, and none of my family had even graduated from college, let alone law school. I'd shoveled manure, castrated hogs, and delivered breached calves with my bare hands. I'd been a member of the Future Farmers of America. True, I had some pretty vicious fights with the farm boys, and nearly killed some of them, but I'd never seen drug dealers, street thugs, or thieves in my life; and I'd never seen a criminal trial, except on television or in the movies. I'd somehow gotten myself into an Ivy League law school, from which I was guaranteed a position with a prestigious law firm and a comfortable living. Yet suddenly here I was, descended into the bowels of a big city, trying to convince people whose lives had been torn apart by drugs, poverty, and crime that I could get them justice and make them happy and whole again. What on earth was I doing here? They looked at me skeptically but hopefully. They were so desperate for help.

The worst thing for me about dealing with crime victims was breaking the news to them that in order to get the justice they wanted, they'd have to relive the original pain of being victimized, first in private with me, and then in public on the witness stand, in front of the person who hurt them. Some of them relished the opportunity to do this, but many of them lost their nerve and said they couldn't bear it. When I explained that I'd have to dismiss their cases and deny them justice, they summoned the courage to go on. They wanted to be happy again. They wanted to be the last one to get justice.

I did my best to help them through it. There were hot tears and words of anguish. Some of their stories were so heartbreaking that tears filled my own eyes and I had to look away. I felt guilty for causing them to remember these things, but I had no choice. Although neither of us realized it at the time, my punishment for dragging them through this was that, by reliving the crimes with them, I became a victim myself. I felt that *my* car had been stolen, that *my* apartment had been burglarized, that *I* had been held up at gun point, that *I* had been savagely beaten. By the time they were through with their stories, I wanted justice as badly as they did. It made me try harder. I wanted to win justice for them *and for myself.*

I won most of the cases I tried, which was a promising start to my legal career. Not that winning was any great feat. Even though as the prosecutor I had the burden of proving the defendant's guilt beyond a reasonable doubt, I had the resources of an entire metropolitan police department to do it. Big city police officers are very good at what they do. Not only do they risk their lives to catch dangerous people on a daily basis, but they gather and analyze all the evidence and then come into court every few weeks to testify about it. This makes them excellent witnesses for a terrified young prosecutor. They're experienced and confident; they know the law and what they need to say under oath to get the job done. Many of them could try cases on their own.

There are so many cases, however, that the police officers can't be expected to remember every detail, and must rely upon the reports they hastily prepared at the time. These reports are often cryptic and incomplete, creating the need to fill in the blanks with memory. Sometimes these blanks are filled in on the witness stand with whatever is necessary to convict the defendant, whether the officer's memory is clear or not. The public defenders know this and attack the officer's recollection on cross examination, but their success is limited because police officers are given great deference by judges and juries. All of which makes for high conviction rates and fast processing of an overwhelming number of cases but which severely damages the innocence and conscience of the terrified prosecutor fresh off the farm.

It isn't only police officers, of course. Victims, defendants, and witnesses wrestle with this too. Memory being imperfect as it is, anyone testifying about the past is prone to filling in the details, which is why witnesses are placed under oath and subject to cross examination—and to prosecution for perjury if they lie. I'm not saying that any of my witnesses ever committed perjury. To my knowledge, not one of them did, although there were times during my career when they wanted to and I wouldn't allow it. But standing there for the first time in a big city courtroom, questioning a police officer whose recollection was failing him, trying with all my might to get justice for the victims sitting behind me but knowing too that the freedom of the defendant sitting at the other table was on the line, the implications of pursuing justice suddenly became for me poignant, wrenching, and real.

For the most part, I was able to put this dilemma out of my mind. Every conviction I won gave me a burst of exhilaration, relief, and pride. The victims would shake my hand and sometimes hug me or cheer. The police officers would wink and slap my back, encouraging me to keep plugging away. The judges would nod their heads approvingly. But then we'd watch the defendant being led away in handcuffs, and we'd realize the case was over and *this* is what we'd won. *This was justice.* The hand shaking and cheering stopped.

It wasn't sympathy for the defendant that soured our victories. It seemed to be sympathy for ourselves. We'd accomplished exactly what we set out to do. The justice system had worked as advertised. The victims and the public had been vindicated. Justice had been served. But after all this cost and effort, could this be our reward, a man being led away in handcuffs? Sure, we found solace in the belief that we'd prevented a future crime by pulling a dangerous person off the streets, but the fact is that that's simply not what the defendant had been put on trial for, or been found guilty of—the likelihood of committing *future* crimes. The defendant had been tried for crimes committed in the *past*, and was being sent to prison as punishment for those crimes. The victims had come to testify not about what the defendant might do to somebody else but about what the defendant had already done to them. Reliving the pain of those events had reopened and irritated the wounds. Seeing the defendant being led away in handcuffs had done nothing to heal them. We actually felt worse. Following every conviction, a grave feeling of foreboding would overcome me that I'd done something terrible . . . not to the defendant necessarily, *but to myself.* Thus, before I'd even passed the bar examination and started my legal career, I began to wonder whether justice causes more suffering than it cures.

I'd heard that the federal judicial system was the place to be as a young attorney because it was considered to be less chaotic and more prestigious than the state courts. So, after law school I applied for and was accepted to become a law clerk to a federal trial court judge. Being a federal law clerk is a highly coveted position among young lawyers. It provides an inside view of the judicial system, unparalleled experience, opportunities to make valuable contacts, and it's considered an important stamp of approval—the attorney equivalent of a physician completing a residency at a renowned teaching hospital or a young priest serving on the staff of an archbishop or a cardinal.

Although I found serving as a federal law clerk to be all these wonderful things and more, my experience only fueled my doubts about the costs and benefits of pursuing justice. A law clerk is the judge's confidential advisor, charged with telling him or her what the law says and recommending how to proceed with and rule on cases that come before the court. The judge always makes the decisions, but law clerks often influence how those decisions are made. The federal judge whom I served was one of the brightest, fairest, and most even-tempered men I've ever known. He took his job very seriously, as did I. When I first met him, he'd just been appointed by the President of the United States to the federal bench from private practice, so I was his first law clerk. We learned our jobs together.

One of the things I discovered very quickly is that sentencing criminal defendants is, by a landslide, the most emotionally grueling part of being a judge or a law clerk. During the trial itself, the lawyers and the jury are primarily responsible for seeing that justice is done. The judge simply makes sure everything goes smoothly and according to the rules. But after a guilty verdict is entered, the weight of that verdict lands squarely on the judge's shoulders. He or she must decide how the defendant is to be punished and for how long. I can't remember a single time when we felt good about it.

Sentencing was always the moment of greatest anguish for the victims, defendants, and their families. Not only did everyone yet again have to experience the pain of the crime, but now all the agonizing details excluded during the trial about the impact of the crime upon the victims, defendants, and their families had to be heard along with it. People broke down in tears in the courtroom. Both sides sent desperate, wrenching letters to the judge, alternately pleading for vengeance or mercy. If the sentence we rendered was too light in the victims' estimation, they'd become disgruntled or enraged. If the sentence we rendered conformed to what they wanted, there'd be a sigh of relief or perhaps even some celebration; but after all the suffering they went through to get to this moment, they seemed to find little real peace or happiness. Once again another defendant would trudge away in handcuffs, presumably for the last time. Justice had been served.

The judge and I rarely spoke when sentencing was over. We were shell-shocked and exhausted. No matter how heinous the defendant's crimes, sentencing a human being to prison—potentially for life—is one of the most distressing things one can do. I can't say what the judge was thinking about all this. As for me, I was wondering why, after all these years, human beings hadn't come up with a better way of behaving and resolving their conflicts. *So this is justice?* I wondered. *What have I gotten myself into?*

I fled from criminal law as fast as I could. My haven was a prominent law firm with branch offices around the world and beautiful offices in a skyscraper overlooking the Philadelphia Art Museum. My client base consisted of a Who's Who list of multinational corporations and wealthy individuals, as well as *pro bono* representation of some very poor clients, among them abused children and indigent prisoners in the Philadelphia prison system seeking better conditions of confinement. I concentrated my practice on complex litigation in most areas of civil law, with an emphasis on environmental law. I worked on trials and appeals in courts across the country. I wrote many legal briefs, appeared at many depositions and hearings, and negotiated many compromises. I was paid very well.

Regardless of the type of client, however, I soon found that whether I won a small motion or an entire case, I wasn't happy for long. A wave of satisfaction and pleasure followed each victory, but it disappeared quickly, leaving me feeling empty but wanting more. Soon, every little battle turned into a big battle as I searched for that satisfaction and pleasure again and again. I became ruthless in my pursuit of justice: filing more lawsuits, working longer hours, behaving more aggressively, sharpening my tactics, attacking ferociously, demonizing the other side and burying them in a grave of pleadings and papers. Letters to opposing counsel became my machine gun fire, depositions became strafing runs, motions became bombing missions, and trials all out thermonuclear war. I'd do virtually anything to win and experience the thrill again. Compassion, decency, and common courtesy were eradicated from my legal practice, and from my personal life as well, because they only stood in the way of my next exhilarating hit of justice.

I had an uneasy feeling about all this, the way I've come to understand some soldiers feel about killing. It wasn't how I'd envisioned life as a lawyer, but I couldn't control it any more than a soldier can control the nature of warfare. This is the way the justice system is designed, like warfare, with winner-take-all outcomes. Sometimes I felt guilty for winning because this meant somebody else had been bloodied and lost. I left behind a trail of vanquished litigants, but I was a casualty too and found myself and my clients convalescing for extended periods of time. Very often, I questioned my tactics for winning and the intricate laws, rules, and judicial opinions that, when mastered, could deliver victory without regard to the so-called "justice" of the outcome. I noticed some of this same uneasiness among my colleagues and opponents as well. Every trial lawyer I knew craved victory, but most of the time, even when winning, every trial lawyer I knew seemed grumpy and miserable.

As I mentioned earlier, at first I thought all this misery was caused by the pressures of legal practice. The demand for justice in our society is so insatiable that the justice system is overtaxed and many lawyers feel overworked. The lawyers who excel at delivering justice are highly sought after, and they're pitted against other lawyers who excel at it, creating the fiercest of battles. Recent studies indicate that lawyers in the United States experience the highest incidence of clinical depression of any occupation: 25 percent of all lawyers were found to be clinically depressed, more than twice the rate in the general population (Johns Hopkins University; Gernader, *Lawyers Concerned for Lawyers*, 57 DEC Bench & B. Minn. 5, 2000). Recent studies also show that 15 percent to 18 percent of attorneys are alcoholics versus 10 percent of the general population (Benjamin, "The Prevalence of Depression, Alcohol Abuse and Cocaine Abuse Among United States Lawyers," 13 *Int'l J.L. & Psychiatry*, 233–34, 1990). The divorce rate among lawyers is also higher than other professionals, and in a recent poll half of all lawyers said they were dissatisfied with their jobs (Seligman, *Authentic Happiness*, Free Press, 2002).

These are grim statistics, for lawyers and for society as a whole. Many articles and books have been written on this phenomenon, with most concluding that lawyer depression, addiction, and dissatisfaction comes from the win-lose aspect of the justice system, long hours, high pressure to succeed, fear of failure, limited family and social life, lack of meaningful choices and client contact, increased competition among lawyers, and a general sense of declining professionalism made manifest in the impoliteness and aggressiveness of other lawyers (Seligman, *Authentic Happiness*). These explanations seemed plausible to me, so after about five years in this pressure cooker, I decided I'd be happier if I looked elsewhere. I found a small law firm that appeared to be ideal. It had a sophisticated legal practice, wealthy clients, great pay, and I could work from home, where I could control my time and be with my wife and young children. It should have been the perfect situation; but even here, with better hours, reduced pressure, direct contact with my clients, and surrounded by my family, I remained miserable. After a few years of this, I became so desperate that I cut my practice back to part time. When I dreaded even four hours a day as an attorney, I knew something was terribly wrong.

Perhaps, I thought, mine was a case of having chosen the wrong profession. Not so long before, being an Episcopal priest had seemed like a match made in heaven. I looked into it again, but it still didn't stir any real passion in me. In the vernacular, I didn't feel "called" to the priesthood. I just felt unhappy about being a lawyer. So I started looking around to see what else I could do with a doctoral degree in jurisprudence. I was good at developing legal strategies, writing briefs, and performing legal research. So, thinking that I could insulate myself from the combat, I founded a company that provided services to other lawyers fighting in the trenches. I even patented a software system to do all this over the Internet (those were the heady days of the Internet boom, when the possibilities seemed endless). My little company fared reasonably well; within a couple of years, we boasted more than one hundred law firms around the country as clients. But this too left me feeling empty and, at risk of sounding repetitive, *miserable.*

It was time to do some serious soul searching.

I looked back over my career to see where I could have possibly gone wrong. It really had been a fairy tale ride from failure as a farm boy to the top of the legal profession. I'd exceeded everyone's expectations, including my own. What was there to complain about? But seeing the big picture, I began to piece together a consistent theme. The more successful I'd become at winning justice, the more my happiness seemed to slip away from me. This was very odd, and very disturbing, because it contradicted everything I'd learned as a child about justice, and everything society teaches us about justice every day.

I dug more deeply into my experiences as a civil lawyer and reflected upon my clients' reactions when I won justice for them. To my surprise, I saw the same phenomenon at work among them as well. Not only was I less happy when I succeeded in winning justice, but, after all the celebrating was over, my clients seemed less happy having it. It was the same thing I'd experienced in the district attorney's office and as a law clerk, but I'd overlooked it in the heat of battle. Regardless of the type of dispute, whether I represented the plaintiff or the defendant, civil litigation ground my clients down emotionally and financially. Like the victims in a criminal case, they were forced to relive over and over— in excruciating detail—all the pain and aggravation of their disagreements with vendors, partners, employers, employees, customers, directors, shareholders, physicians, patients, and families. They grew weary, jaded, and bitter. The temptation for them to shade the truth to win, or even outright lie, was tremendous. When they did win, they delighted in their victories, but within days, hours, or even minutes, they seemed unhappy again. There were new problems with the same adversary, or new adversaries with the same problem. Yet the more successful I was on their behalf, the more they wanted justice to fend off these problems and bad feelings, and with it more bravado from me: more lawsuits and victories, each with its little shimmer of excitement and then its big letdown. Like drug addicts, they were willing to bankrupt themselves emotionally and financially to get more and more justice, which only produced—as difficult as it seemed for me to believe—more and more unhappiness. And like a drug pusher, I kept encouraging them to want it . . . selling it to them by the briefcase.

Drug addicts and drug pushers? I know, none of this made sense to me either. To make matters more confusing, looking back on my legal career, I noticed that my happiness, and my clients' happiness, actually improved in those cases where I was able to negotiate a private compromise with the other side rather than deliver a courtroom knockout. In other words, the less justice I extracted from my clients' relationships, the more happy they were!

And then I uncovered the greatest paradox of all about the practice of law. The best times I ever had as a lawyer—the times when it seemed both my clients and I were the happiest, and when our happiness endured—were the times when I was able to convince my clients that the best thing to do about a dispute was to make amends with the other side as quickly as possible and forget about the whole thing. No demands, no threats, no lawsuits. Either repay the debt or forgive it. Do whatever it takes to end the dispute, even if you receive nothing in return. How could this accomplish anything? Because my clients who tried it always received something unexpected and of far greater value in return—they received peace and happiness.

I was so stunned by these revelations that I began to test them in my personal life to see whether I was understanding things correctly. Sure enough, it was true. The more I used my skills as a lawyer to obtain justice against my wife, family, friends, and the people with whom I did business (and this I did often, like a bully on a playground), the more unhappy I became. Conversely, the more often I compromised with these people, the happier I felt. And I felt happiest of all when I didn't fight the battle in the first place. I felt peaceful and content when I didn't chase the guy who cut me off in traffic, when I didn't chastise the rude waiter, when I didn't try to win the argument with my wife. I was onto something. Something very strange but also something very important.

It caused the greatest crisis of my life.

THREE

The Crisis

There was no making sense of my experiences within the legal profession. Justice was injustice. Success was failure. Up was down. Left was right. I'd spent tens of thousands of dollars and most of my adult life training myself to become a mercenary for justice, but I found myself happier and more useful to my clients when I convinced them to walk away from the fight. How could a lawyer make a living doing that? How could a lawyer even admit this was happening?

I'd constructed my entire life upon the premise that the pursuit of justice would guarantee my happiness. Now I was receiving the message that the pursuit of justice was guaranteeing my *un*happiness. If that message was correct, then it would mean my entire life—and particularly my legal career—had been a tragic mistake. It would mean every step I thought I took forward had been a step backward. It would mean every victory was a loss I hadn't known I'd suffered. It would also mean that large segments of my ancient and venerable profession were flawed in their very conception. And since our country itself is organized upon the principle that justice ensures our happiness, and since we make decisions to jail, execute, and go to war based on this assumption—it would mean we're all making a very big mistake. Because one thing is certain. We all want *happiness* more than anything else in life. If pursuing justice makes our happiness impossible, then we've got some serious rethinking to do.

I had no intention of calling for this type of rethinking. You don't attack the American justice system, the most powerful institution in the most powerful country in the world, on a whim. Nor do you blithely question the assumptions upon which people have based their most important decisions for centuries. And despite my overall dissatisfaction with the practice of law, it had been good to me, and I was fond of thinking of myself as a lawyer. It carries with it a certain amount of respect (and disrespect). Lawyers have made great contributions to the common good throughout history. By nature, we're a conservative lot, generally concerned with laws and rules and getting things right. I've always been this way, which is why I was good at being a lawyer. I've never been one to take half-cocked positions and bring public scorn upon myself. All these years, I'd been quietly doing my job with my necktie pulled tight. I had every intention of keeping it that way.

But I just couldn't get this conflict between justice and happiness out of my mind. My identity as a lawyer seemed at war with my soul. What I was thinking in private was, in modern terms, akin to punishable heresy in ancient times. I was thinking this: *What if the pursuit of justice is evil, not good?* I started questioning my sanity. My family was suffering. I was thoroughly miserable and no longer making a good living. My wife (God bless her, she's a lawyer too) was working full time because of it and not seeing our children as much as she, they, or I wanted. The rest of my family thought I was peculiar, to put it nicely. My lawyer friends were distancing themselves from me—or was it me from them? In the end, I cloistered myself from the rest of the world in a spare room in my house.

Something would have to give.

I had two options. I would either have to abandon my career and my lifelong pursuit of justice, or I would have to embrace it by proving to myself that justice was *good*, not evil, and that pursuing justice was not the source of my unhappiness. Since I was most definitely not willing to give up my legal career, I chose the latter.

This gave me a plan but raised a new question. Where could I go to prove to myself that pursuing justice was not the source of my unhappiness? I was pretty scared by this point. My success and my future were on the line. Who could I talk to about something this important?

Then suddenly the answer seemed obvious.

I would need to go back to the source of my deepest beliefs about justice. And I would need to turn where I had always turned, even as a young child, when I became frightened and desperate. The source of my beliefs and the source of my comfort were one and the same.

I turned to God.

Four

The Spiritual Journey

Something about the spiritual dangers of pursuing justice sounded vaguely familiar to me. I went back to the Bible, back to the lessons my grandfather had preached, back to the teachings I had learned in the Episcopal Church. Sure enough, I discovered that Jesus had spoken about the perils of pursuing justice long ago, in his Sermon on the Mount:

> The law of Moses says, "If a man gouges out another's eye, he must pay with his own eye. If a tooth gets knocked out, knock out the tooth of the one who did it." But I say: Don't resist violence with violence! If you are slapped on one cheek, turn the other too. If you are ordered to court and your shirt is taken from you, give your coat too. If the military demand that you carry their gear for a mile, carry

it two. Give to those who ask, and don't turn away from those who want to borrow.

There is a saying, "Love your friends and hate your enemies." But I say: Love your enemies! Pray for those who persecute you! In that way you will be acting as true sons of your Father in heaven. For he gives his sunlight to both the evil and the good, and sends rain on the just and on the unjust too. If you love only those who love you, what good is that? Even scoundrels do that much. If you are friendly only to your friends, how are you different from anyone else? Even the heathen do that. But you are to be perfect, even as your Father in heaven is perfect (The Living Bible, Matthew 5:38–48).

The fact that my grandfather had preached this lesson seemed curious to me. He was the same guy who preached about the divine necessity of pursuing justice; yet here was Jesus telling us to stay away from it—and claiming that even God Himself, perfect as He is, won't touch it. Weren't these two teachings in direct conflict with each other? How had my grandfather reconciled them?

The answer is they *are* in direct conflict with each other, but my grandfather didn't bother trying to reconcile them—and most followers of Christianity haven't bothered either. This is generally considered to be Jesus' most difficult teaching. Forgiveness like this seems virtually impossible for most folks. We either consider Jesus superhuman to have accomplished it, or we think he was naïve to have suggested it. As a middle ground, we sometimes try to bargain our way out of forgiveness by calling it a mental exercise, something to be done in private while in public we seek retribution with everything we've got.

All three of these answers suited me just fine. I've had

difficulty forgiving people my entire life. My brother, my parents, the farm boys, the criminals I convicted, the litigants I defeated, the people who cut me off in traffic, the rude waiters, my friends, my wife, even myself. . . . Justice was my "A" game in life and I saw little room in it for forgiveness. I assumed forgiveness is something God and Jesus work out between themselves at the end. It held no value for me during this lifetime because it would mean allowing somebody to run away with my happiness, which I was unwilling to permit.

I considered my search for the answer to my dilemma over at this point. The answer was this: It really doesn't matter whether justice causes unhappiness because, even if it does, there's nothing we can do about it anyway. If our only options when we're wronged are pursuing justice or offering forgiveness, then pursuing justice is the only viable response. Period. That's the way life's always been. That's why, two thousand years after Jesus preached his sermon, we still go to war and we still put most of our faith and hope in an unwieldy justice system. It is difficult to reconcile Jesus' teachings consistently with the rest of the Bible, especially the Old Testament preachments about justice, let alone with the realities of life. Theological conflicts are enigmatic, but the world goes on.

So back I went to practicing law. I can't tell you how relieved I was. My legal consulting company grew. I represented a few wealthy clients on the side. I started rejuvenating my connections within the legal community and even dipping my toe into politics. My peace and sanity returned. Money flowed again. What I now chalked up to a midlife crisis had been averted. Everything seemed wonderful.

But God wasn't finished speaking to me.

As time went by, it became more difficult for me to shrug off Jesus' teachings. First, I was having fresh experiences in my personal life that informed me in strident ways that Jesus might have been doing more than telling us to be nice to others so God will be nice to us when we die. The nature of these experiences is unimportant. They were mostly simple aggravations in everyday life and in my legal practice that, when forgotten, didn't cause me problems, but when I pursued justice, blossomed into strife. Each incident seemed freighted with a message that I was supposed to hear about the dangers of pursuing justice.

Second, I found that at an emotional and spiritual level I'd fallen in love with Jesus' words. For reasons I can't explain, I *wanted* them to be true. I wanted them to be reconcilable with reality. I wanted unconditional forgiveness to be possible to achieve. And the more I read the Sermon on the Mount, the more I became convinced that Jesus was trying to tell us that when we don't forgive our enemies—when we pursue justice—we make ourselves unhappy *in this life*, not the afterlife.

This wasn't easy for a lawyer's rational mind to accept. To that mind, forgiveness was something that benefits only the person we forgive—hence the word, "for give." I'd always believed the injunction "to be perfect, even as your Father in Heaven is perfect" means we should give this incredibly gracious gift of forgiveness to this incredibly rotten person who doesn't deserve it—and who deserves to be sued or jailed instead. But what if forgiveness has less to do with gifts for the person being forgiven than it does gifts for ourselves? What if denying ourselves these gifts by pursuing justice is an unwitting form of self-punishment?

Jesus' words still didn't fully click in my mind at a logical level, but I found them irresistible at an emotional level, and my daily experiences were telling me they might be more powerful than I'd ever imagined. Forgiveness might not be an empty gesture after all but rather a very practical law of cause and effect. If we inflict suffering by pursuing justice against others, then we inflict suffering upon ourselves.

This was an intriguing philosophy, but was it true? And if it was, how could we possibly take advantage of it? Forgiveness is surely one of the most difficult things we can attempt as human beings. Pursuing justice is much easier—or so it seems.

The crisis in my life returned with a vengeance, bigger and more threatening than before. My identity, my career, and my future were up for grabs. But too much was at stake now for me to entrust it to one man, even somebody like Jesus. I understood his views on the subject, but Christian leaders and denominations didn't seem to know what to do with them—and certainly didn't apply them with regularity (crusades, inquisitions, wars, executions, etc.). What about other religions? I wondered. What did they say about the pursuit of justice?

Over the years, I'd become curious about other religions and read many of their most important texts. I found them fascinating and, for the most part, compatible with my Christian upbringing. In some cases, such as Buddhism and Hinduism, I'd even adopted a few of their practices. Therefore, I decided to find out what they had to say about the pursuit of justice and see how it squared with Jesus' teachings and my own experiences. What I discovered was fascinating, and I want to share it with you, but first a word of caution. What follows are generalizations based upon my studies of the major sacred texts from each religion and some related commentaries, particularly Huston Smith's excellent and highly accessible treatise *The World's Religions.* There is no attempt here to include all of the potentially infinite number of different beliefs, nuances, and theological positions held by various sects and individuals within each religion; nor, most importantly, is there an intention here to criticize any religion. My goal has been limited to discerning the generally accepted position of each religion on the pursuit of justice. With that caveat, here's what I discovered:

Judaism

I began my search with Judaism and found that it comes down decisively in favor of the pursuit of justice. In his Sermon on the Mount, Jesus characterized the law of Moses as an eye for an eye, and Jesus was, of course, correct in this characterization. The Torah, the Old Testament, is replete with such teachings:

> Thus says the Lord, the God of Israel [to King David]: "You have struck down Uriah with the sword, and have taken his wife to be your wife, [so] I will raise up trouble against you within your own house; and I will take your wives before your eyes, and give them to your neighbor, and he shall lie with your wives in the sight of this very sun. For you did it secretly; but I will do this thing before all Israel. Because you have utterly scorned the Lord, the child that is born to you shall die" (The Living Bible, 2 Samuel 12:9–14).

After reading this and many similar passages, I conducted a full-text computer search for the word "justice" in the Bible to see how many times it appears. In the King James Version, I found "justice" twenty-nine times in the Old Testament but not once in the books of the New Testament, where Christianity begins. In more modern translations of the Bible, I found justice used more than one hundred times in the Old Testament but only a handful of times in the New Testament, and almost never attributed to Jesus. Similarly, the word "vengeance" appears approximately forty times in both ancient and modern translations of the Old Testament, but only three or four times in the New Testament and, of these, only once attributed to Jesus (in the Gospel of Luke, describing the end of days, not counseling vengeance as a practice).

This research made clear to me that the primary fault line between Judaism and Christianity is located directly beneath the courthouse. The holiest days in Judaism are the Ten Days of Awe, beginning with Rosh Hashanah and ending with Yom Kippur. Many Jews believe that on Rosh Hashanah, God writes down in "books" the names of those who will live and those who will die. On Yom Kippur, which means Day of Atonement, the judgment entered in these books is sealed. During the intervening days, we have an opportunity to change the decree through repentance, prayer, and good deeds. Failure to do so means condemnation for Jews; there's no forgiveness absent an act of contrition.

By comparison, the highest holy days in Christianity are the Holy Week, beginning with Palm Sunday and ending with Easter. Most Christians, especially Protestants, believe their sins have been forgiven once and for all—

and that God's pursuit of justice has been ended—by Jesus' sacrificial crucifixion on Good Friday and his resurrection on Easter Day. Those who accept the validity of this act are believed to be forgiven without further effort. Those who don't are believed to be condemned despite their good deeds (and apparently notwithstanding Jesus' teaching of unconditional forgiveness). Thus, for Christians, theologically speaking, forgiveness requires only acceptance of the forgiveness offered by Jesus. No good deeds or acts of contrition are *per se* necessary or, for that matter, effective. Different denominations within Christianity hold different views. Many fundamentalist Christians, for example, tend to advocate the pursuit of justice in both this lifetime and the next—and to rely primarily upon Old Testament teachings, not the words of Jesus, to support this position. Whether this is a fundamentally Christian, or a fundamentally Jewish, belief might be asked.

Islam

Islam, like Judaism, also comes down decisively in favor of the pursuit of justice. One of the main theological concepts of the Koran is the Day of Judgment and the Reckoning, which, like Judaism, involves images of a Divine "book":

> And We have made the night and the day two signs, then. We have made the sign of the night to pass away and We have made the sign of the day manifest, so that you may seek grace from your Lord, and that you might know the numbering of years and the reckoning; and We have explained everything with distinctness.

And We have made every man's actions to cling to his neck, and We will bring forth to him on the resurrection day a book which he will find wide open:

Read your book; your own self is sufficient as a reckoner against you this day (The Koran, 17.12–17.14, M. H. Shakir trans.).

When the sun is covered,
And when the stars darken,
And when the mountains are made to pass away,
And when the camels are left untended,
And when the wild animals are made to go forth,
And when the seas are set on fire,
And when souls are united,
And when the female infant buried alive is asked
For what sin she was killed,
And when the books are spread,
And when the heaven has its covering removed,
And when the hell is kindled up,
And when the garden is brought nigh,
Every soul shall [then] know what it has prepared (81.1–81.14).

For Muslims, there is no forgiveness without action. According to the Prophet Muhammad, salvation must be earned through deeds alone. We reap what we sow. In contrast to the Sermon on the Mount, the Koran teaches reciprocity and punishment for wrongdoing, *jihad* (the concept of a just or righteous war), and defending ourselves against our enemies. Like the King James version of the Jewish Old Testament, a full text computer search of M. H. Shakir's translation of the Koran reveals 28 instances of the word "justice."

The fact that Judaism and Islam—two of the world's old-est and greatest religions—embrace the pursuit of justice suggested to me that I'd been right after all. I could go back to being a lawyer with a clear conscience. But I found this view exceedingly difficult to adopt when swirling around both of these religions was, and continues to be, a cata-clysmic storm of justice-based earthly suffering that threat-ens to pull everyone into it. I'm speaking, of course, about the conflict between the Israelis and the Palestinians. That the two religions most theologically committed to the pur-suit of justice are locked in a nightmarish war over the same small piece of territory in the Middle East, exchanging jus-tice for justice and suicide bomb for helicopter missile, served as a compelling reason for me to continue my spiri-tual research.

Buddhism

I turned next to Buddhism and found that, unlike Judaism and Islam, its tenets come down decisively *against* the pursuit of justice. The Dhammapada, the best loved Buddhist text, teaches us to abandon anger of all kinds:

> Forsake anger, give up pride. Sorrow cannot touch the man who is not in the bondage of anything, who owns nothing.
> He who can control his rising anger as a coachman controls his carriage at full speed, this man I call a good driver: others merely hold the reins.
> Overcome anger by peacefulness: overcome evil by good. Overcome the mean by generosity; and the man who lies by truth. . . .
> The wise who hurt no living being, and who keep

their body under self-control, they go to the immortal NIRVANA, where once gone they sorrow no more (The Dhammapada, 17:221–223, 225, Juan Mascaró trans.).

With teachings like these, it comes as no surprise that Buddhist cultures historically tend to be more peaceful than others. A poignant example of this phenomenon exists in our own time. Compare the way the Dali Lama, the Buddhist leader of Tibet, has reacted to the occupation of his country by China, with the way Yasir Arafat, the Muslim leader of the Palestinians, reacted to the occupation of his country by Israel. Tibetans and Palestinians lost their homelands at about the same time and suffered greatly. Yet without taking sides in either dispute and focusing solely upon the effects of pursuing or not pursuing justice, it's plain to me that the Dali Lama's less angry, less justice-driven approach has resulted in far less overall suffering for his own people and has earned them far greater empathy, support, and respect worldwide than Yasir Arafat's. It's almost impossible to imagine a Tibetan monk as a suicide bomber. As things stand, the path of pursuing justice followed by the Palestinians has not brought them any closer to their goals of returning to their homeland and restoring their happiness than the path of nonviolence pursued by the Tibetans, who share similar goals. To the contrary, the Tibetans seem already to have found peace and happiness, even in exile, whereas the Palestinians continue to suffer grievously from their own violence, paying a terrible price in terms of loss of life, property, dignity, and hope. Similarly, the Israelis continue to pay a high price in terms of loss of life, property, dignity, and hope each time they pursue justice against the Palestinians. These very real consequences of pursuing and not pursuing justice give both immediacy and high definition to their theological underpinnings.

Taoism

I studied Taoism next and found that it too comes down decisively against the pursuit of justice. The *Tao Te Ching* makes the following observations about justice and the use of force:

> I have just three things to teach:
> simplicity, patience, compassion.
> These three things are your greatest treasures.
> Simple in actions and in thoughts,
> you return to the source of being.
> Patient with both friends and enemies,
> you accord with the way things are.
> Compassionate toward yourself,
> you reconcile all beings in the world . . .
>
> When two great forces oppose each other,
> the victory will go
> to the one that knows how to yield . . .
>
> Nothing in the world
> is as soft and yielding as water.
> Yet for dissolving the hard and inflexible,
> nothing can surpass it.
>
> The soft overcomes the hard;
> the gentle overcomes the rigid.
> Everyone knows this is true,
> but few can put it into practice.

Therefore the Master remains
serene in the midst of sorrow.
Evil cannot enter his heart.
Because he has given up helping,
he is the people's greatest help.

Throw away morality and justice,
and people will do the right thing.

True words seem paradoxical (*Tao Te Ching*, 19, 67, 69, 78,
Stephen Mitchell trans.).

Hinduism

Turning next to Hinduism, I found that it acknowledges
the necessity of *mankind* to pursue justice as one of many
paths of evolution, but that this pursuit must be abandoned
if we're ever to approach the face of God.

The Bhagavad-Gita, the most well-known of Hindu texts,
portrays God in the form of Lord Krishna counseling the
warrior Arjuna on the battlefield to do his duty and fight his
enemy. This seems at first like encouragement to pursue justice, but Lord Krishna is instead making the more important point that, in the realm of the Absolute, where there is
only God, death is not possible and therefore there can be
nothing to fear in life—not even death itself:

The truly wise mourn neither for the living nor for
the dead.

There was never a time when I did not exist, nor you,
nor any of these kings [arrayed against you, Arjuna].

Just as the dweller in this body passes through childhood, youth and old age, so at death he merely passes into
another kind of body. The wise are not deceived by that.

Feelings of heat and cold, pleasure and pain, are

caused by the contact of the senses with their objects. They come and they go, never lasting long. You must accept them.

A serene spirit accepts pleasure and pain with an even mind, and is unmoved by either. He alone is worthy of immortality.

That which is non-existent can never come into being, and that which is can never cease to be. Those who have known the inmost Reality know also the nature of *is* and *is not.*

That Reality which pervades the universe is indestructible. No one has power to change the Changeless.

Bodies are said to die, but That which possesses the body is eternal. It cannot be limited or destroyed. Therefore you must fight (Bhagavad-Gita, II, Swami Prabhavanada and Christopher Isherwood trans.).

Why must Arjuna fight? Lord Krishna explains that the outcome of earthly battle has no consequences in the realm of the Absolute, but if Arjuna goes through with it, he can learn this great Truth experientially, for this is his station in life. Arjuna is of the warrior caste, through which, according to Hindu teachings, he must successfully pass if he is to reach Truth. Of those who successfully reach Truth, however, Lord Krishna is clear that the cravings of justice do not pertain and he describes such a person thus:

He knows bliss in the Atman [the Eternal]
And wants nothing else.
Cravings torment the heart:
He renounces cravings.
I call him illumined.

Not shaken by adversity,
Not hankering after happiness:

> Free from fear, free from anger,
> Free from the things of desire.
> I call him a seer, and illumined (II).

These are powerful words. Mahatma Gandhi, the spiritual father of civil disobedience and nonviolence, regarded the Bhagavad-Gita "as the book *par excellence* for the knowledge of Truth." He made this declaration in the same chapter of his autobiography in which he reflected upon his first time reading Jesus' Sermon on the Mount, which he said "went straight to my heart."

That Gandhi had been a lawyer before becoming a spiritual leader astonished me. Here was a modern man of such piety and power that he defeated the entire British empire without a gun. He was India's George Washington, but he never led an army or raised a sword. He proved there is a nonviolent means to achieve revolutionary ends. Yet, as mentioned earlier, he said his regard for jurisprudence increased as he made the transition from lawyer to religious leader because he "discovered in it religion."

Gandhi's words gave me great hope. I'm not aware that Gandhi spoke directly about the perils of pursuing justice, but, as was also mentioned earlier, he left behind for us this telling observation at the end of his autobiography: "To see the universal and all-pervading Spirit of Truth face to face one must be able to love the meanest of creation as oneself."

Confucianism

Finally, I turned to Confucius and, as with Hinduism, found split teachings. To the question "Should one love one's enemy, those who do us harm?" Confucius answered in direct opposition to Jesus: "By no means. Answer hatred with justice, and love with benevolence. Otherwise you would waste your benevolence" (as quoted in Smith, *The World's Religions*). This would seem to place Confucius squarely in the company of Moses and Muhammad.

On the other hand, Confucius is credited with invoking the Silver Rule: "Do not do unto others what you would not want others to do unto you" (VII, *The Analects of Confucius*). Confucius' concepts of *Jen* (benevolence, love, and human-heartedness) and *chun tzu* (Superior Person) posit the ideal human being as one who expresses empathy, charity, and magnanimity toward others and who knows that "within the four seas all men are brothers and sisters." When asked by a ruler whether the lawless should be executed, Confucius answered: "What need is there of the death penalty in government? If you showed a sincere desire to be good, your people likewise would be good. The virtue of the prince is like the wind; the virtue of people like grass. It is the nature of grass to bend when the wind blows upon it." This statement suggests, to me at least, Confucius' understanding that the pursuit of justice is a last resort—a sign of failure by society and its leaders to live and lead rightly, not merely a sign of immorality among evildoers. Thus, like Hinduism, Confucianism seems to regard the pursuit of justice as a sometimes necessary but altogether inferior response to be set aside as we spiritually mature.

Tallying the justice score on the world's religions, I found two in favor of the pursuit of justice, three against, and two that consider justice a legitimate but inferior pursuit to be abandoned if we are "to see the Spirit of Truth face to face."

My studies provided me with invaluable insight but no clear answer to my dilemma. In the final analysis, support can be found in the great religious texts for pursuing both justice and forgiveness. Indeed, this is exactly what humanity has done as a matter of expedience. When we wish to pursue justice against each other, we cite those passages that support it and ignore the teachings about forgiveness. Conversely, when we wish to be peaceful in the face of injustice, we cite the teachings about forgiveness and ignore the teachings about justice. Both paths can be "justified."

But what if someone were determined to discover the real truth about pursuing justice, rather than invoking and revoking it when convenient? Where could one go to learn the true implications of pursuing justice versus forgiveness?

I dove even deeper into the spiritual world to find out.

FIVE

The Awakening

So tormented was I by these contradictions among religious teachings, and within my own experience, that I decided to take matters into my own hands. I began to write a novel in which I could play out the conflict between justice, forgiveness, and happiness at a safe distance.

I entitled this novel *NEVAEH* (the word "heaven" spelled backwards), and in it I set out to discover what it might be like to be a lawyer in the afterlife, representing souls at the Final Judgment. What if, I imagined, this lawyer of souls had found her way into the afterlife after being murdered (to keep things at an even safer distance, I made my hero Brek Cuttler, a woman and a young mother). And what if once there she met the soul of the man who murdered her and was forced to choose between prosecuting and defending him? What if she discovered that *her* soul had been on trial all along, not his?

There it was, in all its terrifying glory, the conflict I'd been struggling with since my final year in law school, but set in the spiritual world where I feared it had been unfolding all along.

One of the wonderful things about writing a novel is that you have the opportunity to play God and create an entire world. One of the difficulties is that, as God, you must figure out for yourself how the main conflict finds resolution. The real God of our world may have created it in a week, but finishing *NEVAEH* took me ten years.

As my writing neared the end, the moment of truth arrived for my dear colleague and alter ego, Brek Cuttler, Esq. What would she do? I panicked because I realized I'd actually compounded my problem. Now, not only was *my* personal and professional life on the line, but this woman's soul hung in the balance. I'm only being half-facetious. I was distraught, but I confess that I knew all along how the conflict in the novel would be resolved. I wrote those final chapters with tears of joy and exaltation streaming down my face, ending the book the way it had begun, in Brek's own words after the verdict had been reached on her soul:

> I do not remember anymore.
>
> Were my eyes blue like the sky or brown like fresh-tilled earth? Did my hair curl into giggles around my chin or drape over my shoulders in a frown? Was my skin light or dark? Was my body heavy or lean? Did I wear tailored silks or rough cotton and flax?
>
> I do not remember. I remember that I was a woman, which is more than mere recollection of womb and bosom. And for a moment, I remembered all my

moments in linear time, which began with womb and bosom and ended there too. But these are fading away now, discarded ballast from a ship emerged from the storm. I do not mourn the loss of any of these; nor am I any longer capable of mourning. . . .

I remember hearing the sounds of water rushing and wind blowing, of dolphins laughing and birds singing, of children talking and parents sighing, of stars and galaxies living and dying—all the sounds of the earth breathing, if you could have heard it from the other side of the universe. I remember hearing God in those sounds, crying out for forgiveness from Cudi Dagh, and I remember hearing humanity in those sounds, crying out for forgiveness from Golgotha. And there too in the music was the ineffable joy of Noah, reaching up from the littoral to forgive his Father, and above that the ineffable joy of God, reaching down from the cross to forgive his children. And somewhere still, more faint but it was there, I heard the cry of Otto Rabun Bowles, and with it the song of another soul, so joyous it could be heard above all these sounds, singing three words over and over:

"I AM LOVE! I AM LOVE! I AM LOVE!"

It was the song of unconditional love—the song of Eve returning home to the Garden after such a long and terrifying journey. The song grew louder as the presentation of my life continued, and in this song I heard divine perfection, because in it I heard all of Creation: my birth into the world was in that song and my mother's first embrace; flowers were there, and music, and sun and rain, mountains and oceans, books and paintings; boyfriends and girlfriends were there, brothers and sisters on porch swings, children at play in sandboxes, a young man running to the defense of a woman; horses, sailboats, apple trees and cattle were there, and mothers nurturing their young, and bread and water, eyes and ears, skin and hair, lips and arms and legs; air was there, and water and blankets, sunsets, moons and stars, work and play, heroes and heroines. The generations were in that song, and generosity and selflessness too. And love was there. But fear was there also: a parent's abusiveness and a child's selfishness, a dishonest lawyer and her dishonest client, an adulterer and his lover, a soldier and his gun, a death chamber and an incinerator, racists, liars, drunks, rapists, and thieves. Boys who tortured crayfish were in this song, and the God who slaughtered his own children and the children who slaughtered their own God; but even this sounded sweet, because out of it came the light—the light and gift of God.

After I wrote these words, I blessed Brek Cuttler for her courage and wisdom, and God for the inspiration to create her. But what was driving me to despair was that despite knowing how to resolve the conflict for Brek, I still didn't know how to do it for myself—and whether there'd be tears of joy or sorrow at the end.

At about this time, I came upon the story of George Fox who in 1647 was driven to despair by similar questions and found relief not in religious texts but in a direct spiritual revelation, with a voice from nowhere saying to him: "There is one, even Christ Jesus, that can speak to thy condition." Fox went on to found the Religious Society of Friends (Quakers). Quakers are the small mystical sect of Christianity known best for their peace testimony, silent Meetings for Worship, and excellent schools and universities. They're also the only religious organization to be awarded the Nobel Peace Prize, in 1947.

Sufficiently intrigued, I sought out a Quaker meeting to see whether I too might receive direct Divine guidance for my "condition." Since I lived in southeastern Pennsylvania, where William Penn had established Quakerism in North America, there were many quaint old Quaker meeting-houses throughout the countryside, although I had no idea whether any of them were still in use. I selected one nearby and found some cordial, spiritually sophisticated people there. They welcomed me into the silence, which seemed to flow from a deep well of power, akin to Buddhist meditation but punctuated with shared Christian insights. Disappointingly, I didn't hear the voice that had spoken to George Fox during these meetings, but I did discover that Quaker worship suited me and I kept attending.

One Sunday morning, when my distress over the conflict between justice and happiness had reached its peak (and when my audacity knew no further bounds), I tried to force God to speak to me by standing before the Meeting and placing justice on trial. I asked the members of the Meeting to be the jury and made out my case, explaining how the pursuit of justice had produced unhappiness in my life and throughout the history of mankind. I spoke passionately of things both recent and long ago, of victims and vengeance, suffering and joy, and of the nobility, hope, and folly of the human race. It was, I thought, my greatest moment as a lawyer, a page lifted from *The Devil and Daniel Webster* albeit with considerably less style. When I finished, I sat down in the silence to receive the verdict, convinced that an end to my suffering was surely at hand. But to my deep dismay, no verdict came. I found instead a hung jury and was forced to declare a mistrial. It seems that even modern Quakers—the most peace-loving of Christians—are as divided as the world's religions about the merits of pursuing justice.

Still the questions burned, and I plunged even deeper

into the mysterious Light of the spiritual world, meditating, praying, and beginning a second novel, this one exploring the conflict between justice and forgiveness in this life, rather than the afterlife. I reread the sacred texts of the world's religions and revisited many of the great works of literature that struggle with similar questions (*War and Peace, The Brothers Karamazov, Siddhartha, Saint Joan, East of Eden, To Kill a Mockingbird, The Kingdom of God Is Within You, The Fountainhead*). I read nonfiction works (*The World's Religions, The Power of Myth,* and *The Unconquerable World*). I even read more controversial texts like the Gnostic Gospels, *Conversations with God,* and *A Course in Miracles.* I found great truth and comfort in all of these books, but still peace eluded me.

In the middle of writing my second novel and reading *A Course in Miracles,* I slipped beyond the point of despair and into the bitter resignation that I'd never receive the answers to what I believed were among the most important questions about human existence and finish my life with its greatest conflict unresolved. Thus I entered the Christian Lenten season of 2004 depressed, discouraged, and alone, convinced that all my efforts had come to naught and that my life had gotten so far off track I'd never get it back. I was angry with God for allowing me to stray so widely, and to give up so much, all for nothing. As the dark days of Lent progressed, my bitterness eventually turned into submission, and my submission eventually turned into acceptance. I abandoned the struggle to find the answers, succumbing to the possibility that the questions themselves had been wrongly put and that the conflict tormenting me had been a fiction created by my mind.

It was during the bleakest hour of perhaps the bleakest day of my life, when I'd been emptied of all pride, stripped of all logic and reason, purged of all pretensions and pre-conceptions, and left bare before God that something of a miracle happened. Instead of the physical and emotional collapse I'd anticipated (and, in a perverse way, longed for), I experienced the sudden spiritual awakening I spoke about at the beginning of this book. A torrent of energy surged through me, keeping me awake for days on end, bidding me to see, listen, and understand. In this quite unexpected and remarkable way, I received astonishing new clarity and insight into the relationship between justice and happiness. During a period beginning two weeks before Easter 2004 and lasting two weeks after, I was able to distill this new understanding into five teachings about the true nature of justice and happiness—teachings that offer a powerful new way to resolve our conflicts and restore happiness . . . *without lawyers, guns, or money.*

The following chapters contain these five teachings on justice and happiness. In them, you'll find everything you need to resolve the conflicts in your life, together with simple step-by-step instructions for applying the teachings to your specific situation and restoring your happiness *right now.* You'll be invited to submit your disputes for immediate resolution to a free and always-open court of Divine creation. There, you'll be shown how to "sue for peace" anytime, anywhere that conflicts arise. You'll learn what to do and what not to do when you've been wronged, to win back your happiness immediately. Finally, you'll find answers to the questions you've always had about why human beings hurt each other and what can be done to stop it.

There's so much here, it's an embarrassment of riches really. Peace and happiness contain everything, do they not? And are they not exactly what you've been searching for? Are they not the reason you've picked up this book? Well, the time has now arrived for you to have them, in infinite supply. Are you ready?

Then let's get started.

May the words that follow bring you everlasting peace and joy.

The First Teaching:
The Cause of Human Suffering

I have two stories to tell. They're ancient stories, and you've heard them before, but they're also the source of much of our confusion about justice and happiness. Because they've been misunderstood for so long, we need to listen to them again, very carefully this time, so that now we understand their meaning and our happiness can be restored.

The first is the story of Cain and Abel. In this story, Adam and Eve were the first two human beings on earth, and Cain was their first child and Abel their second. Cain grew up to become a farmer and Abel a shepherd. At harvest time, Cain and Abel wanted to impress God with the fruits of their labor. Cain offered God a gift of his produce and Abel offered the fatty cuts of meat from his best lambs. God was pleased with Abel's gift but less so with Cain's. Cain became furious. He'd toiled in the fields all season long, yet here was his younger brother, a shepherd, receiving all God's praise.

Like most children when siblings garner a parent's attention, Cain felt his happiness had been taken from him. Also like most children, Cain was convinced his happiness would be restored if he pursued justice against his brother—or perhaps against God. God warned him against it: "Why are you angry?" God asked. "Why is your face so dark with rage? It can be bright with joy if you will do what you should! But if you refuse to obey, watch out. Sin is waiting to attack you, longing to destroy you. But you can conquer it!"

Cain wouldn't listen. So strong was his craving for justice that he tricked Abel into going out into the fields with him and stabbed him to death. As a result, Cain spent the rest of his life wandering from place to place, a fugitive despised by others and himself.

Now, before we go any further, it doesn't matter in the least whether you believe this story is myth or fact. The truth of its message remains the same in either case. Regardless of how literally or metaphorically we may wish to read the story, we must accept the fact that Cain murdered his brother to get justice. He believed Abel had taken his happiness and that he could get it back by taking Abel's happiness from him. We must also accept that Cain's happiness was *not* restored this way. As God warned him, pursuing justice led only to his own suffering.

This archetypal story appears at the very beginning of

the Bible, a book written thousands of years ago that many believe contains God's Holy Word. In this story, the third human being on the planet murdered the fourth human being. Only one generation avoided the scourge of justice. Yet we still believe today that pursuing justice will restore our happiness. How is this possible after all these years?

The story of Cain and Abel is the story of the dangers of seeking justice.

Another warning about justice appears in the Bible just one chapter later. As if to make absolutely certain we would not overlook or misinterpret it, this story is also the most terrifying in the entire Bible. In it, we see that not even *God* can avoid the dangers of pursuing justice. It's the story of the Great Flood. Again, whether you believe this story is myth or fact is irrelevant. The truth of its message remains the same in either case.

After Cain murdered Abel, the human population exploded across the earth, but the people began engaging in all sorts of debauchery. God warned them to change their ways, but they wouldn't listen. Finally, in frustration, God said: "My Spirit must not forever be disgraced in man." With these words, God unleashed the rains and flooded the earth in an attempt to destroy mankind itself. With the exception of Noah's family and two of each species, all life on earth was exterminated.

Here we have the earliest story of capital punishment and mass murder. Here we have the first genocide, the first Holocaust—*all perpetrated by God Himself.* This is by far the ugliest, most sadistic, and shocking story in the Bible—and in all of human history—yet we focus upon every aspect of it but this. We glorify Noah's obedience; we dream of what the planks of the ark looked like; we have our children play with the animals; we even convince ourselves that what God did (mass murder, remember?) was justified and conjure in it the beauty of rainbows. Why do we engage in these distractions? To avoid confronting the difficult facts of the story and the important lesson it would have us learn. The facts of the story are these: God was displeased with the evil doings of man. God believed His happiness had been taken from Him. God believed His happiness would be restored by taking our happiness (our lives). *God wanted justice.*

Since everything God does is perfect, even God's justice is perfect. Thus, not only were all evildoers drowned, but the very possibility of evil itself was drowned along with them because there was nobody left on earth to be evil. Can you think of a better definition of "perfect justice"?

But the story doesn't end there. Like the story of Cain and Abel, the story of the Great Flood concludes with a grim warning about the consequences of seeking justice. When the waters receded and God looked upon the utter devastation He had wrought, God learned the lesson that *perfect justice produces perfect unhappiness.* By eliminating the possibility of evil, God had also eliminated the possibility of love, because there was no one left on earth to love or to be loved. In other words, by pursuing perfect justice, God had made His own happiness impossible.

"Never again!" God swore, no matter how wicked people become.

We, however, have not made this promise to ourselves. To the contrary, we stand poised at this very moment to commit what the story accuses God of committing. The promise of "perfect justice" is balanced on the tips of our nuclear warheads, waiting to unfold all its horrifying and illusive glory when we believe our national happiness has been taken.

> *The story of the Great Flood is the story of the dangers of seeking perfect justice.*

Indeed, the story of the Great Flood shows us that perfect justice comes at a price not even God can afford.

Instead of reading these ancient stories as warnings to stay away from justice, as they were plainly intended, we've become so fascinated with justice that we've interpreted them as a *mandate* to pursue it. The Bible is filled with appalling examples of the error of such thinking, all perpetrated by humans in God's name to conceal our own thirst for vengeance. We've even convinced ourselves that God wants us to pursue justice against each other, that God actually pursues justice the way we do, that "Vengeance is [God's]," and that God has created a terrifying place called hell where justice is served for all eternity. Think about that for a moment. If hell is the place where "justice is served" for all eternity, is justice really something we want to be involved with here on earth?

The word "justice" has two very different meanings. As we most often use the word today, the pursuit of justice is synonymous with the pursuit of revenge and retribution. It represents the win-lose idea underlying most of our disagreements, lawsuits, violence, and wars. It signifies the belief that whenever we've been wronged, our peace and happiness can be restored only by taking peace and happiness back from the person who wronged us—as though peace and happiness were commodities of limited supply, like gold and silver, that can be stolen and retrieved. This is the so-called "justice" of our legal systems and our militaries, our playgrounds and our streets, our parents and our children, our teachers and our terrorists, our leaders and our criminals. This truly is the justice of hell.

The other meaning of justice, which we would rather not be reminded of, is the direct opposite of all this and is synonymous with fairness, equity, and righteousness. This form of justice recognizes no differences among people but rather acknowledges that *all* people must be treated with dignity and respect, without winners or losers and without regard to what has happened in the past. This form of justice recognizes that peace and happiness are available to all people in infinite supply because peace and happiness come from within not without, and therefore cannot be taken from us. This is the justice of mercy, love, and forgiveness and, hence, the highest and truest form of justice. *This* is the justice of God, and it knows nothing of vengeance nor demands payment or sacrifice of anyone. God's justice knows of only one thing, and that is unconditional love.

Jesus and many others have tried to correct our misconceptions about justice. He made his teachings on the subject very clear, despite our attempts to confuse them. He provided beautiful examples in his own life so we could see their power. *Jesus demonstrated that the path to achieving happiness is by never pursuing justice—as we use the term.* This message is present in all the world's religions (including Judaism and Islam, both of which find their roots in the same Old Testament stories of Cain and Abel and the Great

Flood). Yet despite all these examples, teachings, and stories, we insist upon pursuing justice—and persist in wondering why we're so unhappy.

The time has come to learn once again about the true relationship between justice and happiness; for we will not find happiness until we have understood. Here it is, once again, as plainly as it can be stated:

The pursuit of justice is the **cause** *of human suffering, not the antidote.*

The record of humanity is developed enough for us to see the truth of this statement. Look back upon our history. You will discover that the pursuit of justice has been the source of every violent, hurtful, and unkind thought, word, and deed since the beginning of time. Whenever somebody does something that threatens, hurts, or embarrasses us, or whenever somebody is different from us or has more than us, our happiness seems to have been taken, and we want it back. *We want justice.* And there's no depth to which we're unwilling to go to get it: nuclear annihilation, genocide, war, terrorism, murder, suicide, torture, slavery, imprisonment, kidnapping, rape, arson, theft, assault, adultery, child abuse, exile, deportation, slander, defamation, perjury, insults, frauds, betrayals, feuds, lawsuits, foreclosures. . . .

We've been very creative.

But wait, you say, how can rapists, arsonists, thieves, child abusers, and adulterers be said to be pursuing justice? The answer may surprise you.

Throughout history, people have offered thousands of reasons for committing their unloving acts, but behind every one of those reasons lies the pursuit of justice. Most rapists, for example, believe their happiness was taken from them by being raped themselves or by being denied love or sexual gratification in their lives. It just isn't fair for so many attractive, happy people to be running around and the rapist not able to possess them and their happiness. Whether rapists know their victims in advance or not is irrelevant. All women (or men, or children) have by their very sexual identities wronged them, and it's time now to even the score. The victim who resists is the one who's wronging them at the moment. Justice demands that the rapist take what he wants.

Some arsonists believe they were wronged and their happiness taken by financial troubles. It's only fair for the insurance company to restore their happiness—after all, they paid the premiums. Or perhaps they believe it's unfair for somebody to have a home nicer than theirs. Or, if they're a firefighter, perhaps they believe it's unfair to be denied the excitement of fighting a fire tonight. Justice demands that the arsonist torch the building.

The thief believes she has been wronged and her happiness has been taken because she doesn't have the nice car, or because the store charges so much for the beautiful purse. The car owner and the store owner can obviously afford new ones: why shouldn't they restore her happiness? Justice demands that the thief steal the property.

The child abuser believes he has been wronged and his happiness has been taken because his child is so unappreciative, demanding, and insolent. The child has embarrassed him or caused him to stop what he was doing to clean up a mess. Or perhaps he himself was abused as a child. Now is his chance to restore his happiness. Justice demands that the abuser beat the child.

The adulterer believes she has been wronged and her happiness has been taken by being forced to live with a man who is no longer pleasant or appealing. Here's another man who's exciting, attractive, and willing to restore her happiness. Justice demands that the adulterer consummate the affair.

Whether the perpetrators of these acts were actually wronged by anyone is quite beside the point. They *believe* they were wronged, and therefore justice demands, or at least permits or excuses, their own wrongful conduct. Thus the following truth:

At the root of every injustice lies the pursuit of justice.

Don't believe me? Think for a moment of some of the hurtful things you've done to others during your life. Were you not convinced at the time that your happiness had been taken and that you somehow had the "right" to take theirs? Were you not convinced that the other person had it coming? Were you not convinced that justice demanded, or at least excused, your actions? Now recall some of the hurtful things others have done to you. Do you doubt that these people were convinced they had the right, that you had it coming, and that they were acting in the name of justice— however wrong you believe they were? If you retaliated against them, was your retaliation not also in the name of justice? And did this not beget further retaliation from them in the name of justice? It's a vicious cycle indeed, one that never seems to end. Each act of justice—which seems only fair play at the time—creates more suffering and the demand for more justice.

Why? Because there's no objective standard or limit for

getting justice, and because the desire for justice increases as the experience of happiness decreases. Like one's perception of happiness, one's perception of justice is purely subjective and always in the eye of the beholder. This means that one person's justice is always another person's injustice . . . because the entire goal of getting justice is to take away another person's happiness. Thus, the more we seek justice, the more we create injustice.

But if justice causes so much suffering in our world, why do we want it so badly?

I'm glad you asked.

SEVEN

The Second Teaching:
The Justice Addiction

We have created a world that worships justice as a religion, a world where the most sacred mantras of public discourse are "justice has been served," "bring them to justice," "do justice," "I want justice," "demand justice," "no justice—no peace," and "just war." We have created a world in which schoolchildren kill each other for justice, adults engage in every form of malice in the name of justice, terrorists indiscriminately massacre thousands of people under the delusions of justice, and nations go to war waving the blood-red flag of justice. We have created a world where we expend huge amounts of our resources on the maintenance of justice systems that institutionalize our relentless pursuit of justice.

Why?

Because we believe we can get our happiness back by taking happiness from the person who wronged us. When we say we've been wronged, what we're really saying is that our happiness has been taken away. We feel pain when this happens, and we'll do just about anything to stop it and feel good again. This feeling of pain comes from our perception of being separated, unaccepted, and unloved.

More than anything else in the world, we want to be loved. Because being loved is what makes us happy.

Understand this well, for it applies to all. The rich person and the poor person, the movie star and the adoring public, the athlete and the fanatic, the politician and the voter, the soldier and the enemy, the police officer and the bank robber, the abusive husband and the abused wife, the bully and the classmate, the suicide bomber and the victim, the sinner and the saint—all these people want nothing more than to be loved. Only love makes human beings happy. This is why we are who we are and why we do what we do.

When we've been wronged, we believe we're no longer loved. We feel unaccepted, disrespected, separated, and alone. This makes us intensely unhappy. We're in agony.

So, what exactly are our options for making ourselves feel better at a time like this? In other words, when we've been wronged, how can we make ourselves feel loved, accepted, safe, respected, and reunited again?

Science and medicine have been unable to produce a pill or a therapy that accomplishes this, and they never will, for this type of pain is neither physical nor emotional. It is a spiritual pain, born of what we perceive to be our separation from each other and God. For a pain such as this, we have only two options: we can either pursue justice and try to take our happiness back from the person who took it, or we can pursue forgiveness and try to restore our happiness from within. Those are our only two choices. As a people, we've searched high and low for more. We've enacted laws and created religions; we've explored the physical and mental worlds; we've engaged in every form of diversion and ingested every type of substance. But in the end, we must accept the fact that Cain had only two choices when his gift was rejected by God; and God had only two choices when His creation was debased by man. Likewise, I had only two choices when the farm boys rebuffed me, and my parents had only two choices when they disappointed each other. For the same reasons, a woman abused by her husband has only two choices; a man fired from his job has only two choices; a child molested by an adult has only two choices; a people driven from its country has only two choices; and a nation attacked by terrorists has only two choices.

Of these two choices, we've found the affirmative act of forgiveness to be a sweet sentiment but ultimately unsatisfying and virtually impossible to achieve. To look at the person who has just hurt you and say, "Forget about it, you're forgiven," is something that seems far beyond our capacity most of the time. We think people like Jesus who taught unconditional forgiveness were either God or crazy. Given the choice between justice and forgiveness, we prefer justice.

Again, we do this because we believe we can get our happiness back this way. Otherwise, why bother? Seeking justice requires tremendous effort, involves great personal danger, costs huge sums of money, and risks further retaliation in the name of justice. As we've seen, justice is the primary cause of human suffering and the root cause of the most terrible events in human history. With all these things going against it, we must be convinced that justice will make us feel better and that the benefits outweigh the costs.

Unless, of course, we're behaving irrationally, which we often do. For example, we know that the costs of narcotics and alcohol outweigh the benefits, but millions are addicted to them anyway, convinced the next hit or the next drink will be the one to erase the pain. "But addiction is a physical illness!" you say, not a choice. Fine. But what if the same can be said of justice? What if we're addicted (physically or otherwise) to the very thing that threatens to destroy us and we don't even know it?

To see whether this is true, let's begin by comparing the benefits and costs of seeking justice:

Benefits of Seeking Justice	Costs of Seeking Justice
Vindication	Human suffering
Self-esteem	Personal danger
Commiseration	High financial cost
Deterrence	High social cost
Feeling of Winning	High effort
	High risk of retaliation

Like the highs of narcotics and the lows of alcohol, there's no denying the attractive painkilling effects of justice. With justice, we receive an immediate infusion of vindication and self-esteem. When we're feeling separated and unloved, this sure feels good. We also take comfort from knowing that the people who hurt us are now suffering as well. If we're going to be unhappy, it helps to have company. We feel a little less alone.

The question is whether these effects are only temporary, like the effects of narcotics and alcohol, or whether the pain of being wronged has been cured for good. Another question is whether the benefits of justice outweigh the exceptionally high costs. Take a look at the list again. Justice is by far the most expensive drug you can buy. It had better be long lasting, and it had better be good.

We already know the answer to both questions from personal experience. Justice is only a temporary high and a quick fix. We experience an incredible boost when we inject it, but it wears off quickly, leaving us feeling more miserable than before. Almost immediately after we take our hit, we find ourselves trapped in an escalating war where each person is convinced the other is behaving unjustly and that more justice is needed. We also discover that the pain of the original injustice has returned again with a vengeance, because to summon the energy necessary to pursue justice, we've had to force ourselves to relive the original pain over and over, magnifying it rather than reducing it, goading ourselves on. As the pain increases, we crave another hit and another—like crazed addicts. In the final stages, we find ourselves wracked with guilt and remorse for having behaved so stupidly and so viciously, so that now we're are not only seeking justice against our enemies *but against ourselves.*

Never again! we say. Never again to war! Never again to genocide! Never again to spousal and child abuse! Never again to school killings! Never again to fights with our families, neighbors, and friends!

Until, that is, the next time we feel wronged and the craving for justice returns.

No, justice doesn't make us happy. And justice, the way we use the term, can never make us happy; because justice as vengeance is the opposite of love, making it almost impossible for us to be loved. Justice like this increases separation and intensifies hatred. The meager benefits justice affords come nowhere near outweighing the costs. The fleeting sensations of self-esteem, winning, and vindication, and the fleeting comfort of knowing we're not suffering alone, simply aren't worth the price of our peace and happiness. And deterrence? Really? By focusing on wrongs that occurred in the past, justice is the crudest method of all for preventing future wrongdoing. More often than not, the pursuit of justice results in a future retaliatory act more severe than the first and demanding more justice. More importantly, as we've seen, pursuing justice is what causes wrongdoing in the first place. Seeking it ourselves is like telling a child that stealing is wrong, but then turning around and stealing from him and telling him it's OK—*because you did it, not him.* Seeking justice is what makes terrorists terrorize and murderers murder. How did we ever come to believe that seeking it ourselves would be an effective way of stopping them—without becoming terrorists and murderers ourselves? Experience proves just the opposite. If justice is so effective at preventing future acts of injustice, why did not all wrongdoing in the world end with the "justice" of Cain killing Abel? Why are people being murdered, raped, and assaulted every day despite the $648 billion we invest each year in our justice systems? Why are we still living in a world torn by injustice, war, crime, and violence? Why, in the final analysis, are we not happy?

If we want to stop people from hurting one another, we must show them how to stop seeking justice against one another.

But this hasn't been easy to do—because we're literally *addicted* to pursuing justice. Scientists have recently discovered that when we feel wronged, there's a burst of activity in the same part of the brain that's activated when we're preparing to satisfy hunger and other cravings (*New York Times,* July 24, 2004). In other words, biologically speaking, we seek justice for the same reasons we eat chocolate—to experience pleasure. But like all such cravings, if we indulge them to excess, we experience tremendous suffering and yet stimulate an insatiable desire for more—just as we experience tremendous suffering and yet an insatiable desire for more by indulging biological cravings for alcohol and narcotics. Unfortunately, the suffering experienced by satisfying our justice cravings is far more acute and widespread than that created by feeding chemical addictions. Terrorists and murderers don't only ruin their own lives; they take others with them—sometimes hundreds or thousands of people. When entire societies indulge their cravings for justice, human suffering is experienced on a massive, worldwide scale. War results and millions die. Thus we can see the truth in the following statement:

Justice is the cruelest addiction of all. The very thing we believe will save us is the very thing that's destroying us.

So powerful is the justice addiction that satisfying it has become one of the primary goals of our society. From the time we're born, and throughout the rest of our lives, justice is taught to us and pushed upon us. Our parents, siblings, friends, teachers, and leaders all pursue justice with great passion. Literature, art, history, movies, music, radio, and television are awash in the siren song of justice. We're taught to admire people who excel at obtaining justice and label them heroes. We're encouraged to deride those of gentle spirit who forgive and label them weak. Some of our religions have become so corrupted by this addiction that they actually preach the pursuit of justice as a virtue, something to be perfected and emulated. We've established justice systems that purport to guarantee our happiness but only ensure our unhappiness and, in the process, like drug cartels, create an unquenchable demand for themselves. We've convinced ourselves that lawyers and judges—the priests and prophets of our justice religion—are required to resolve our disputes and restore our happiness. We've persuaded ourselves that if lawyers and judges aren't available, or if we can't afford them, or if their remedies are inadequate, of if we simply can't wait, then guns and bombs are a reasonable substitute. In this insane environment, it's no surprise that most of us grow up not only to become justice addicts but justice pushers. We can't seem to help ourselves.

Know this about the world in which we live:

Drug addicts don't build weapons of mass destruction.
Only justice addicts do.

EIGHT

The Third Teaching:
The Most Important Trial of Your Life

In a world addicted to that which would destroy it, where the pursuit of justice threatens our happiness and our very survival, consider carefully what I am about to say:

The trial of your enemies is the most important trial of your life.

You face this trial over and over again, almost daily throughout your life. Each time it begins, you must choose how it will proceed and how it will end. Will you pursue justice or happiness? Will you yield to your addiction and take the path of suffering? Or will you search for another way?

Your freedom is at stake during this trial, not your enemy's.

The outcome of this trial will determine *your* peace and happiness, and the peace and happiness of your family, nation, and the world. Whether tragedies are avoided or attracted, whether relationships are nurtured or destroyed, whether children are loved or abused, whether degrees are conferred or denied, whether jobs are found or lost, whether illness is prevented or induced, whether discrimination is conquered or encouraged, whether property is protected or stolen, whether a punch is withheld or thrown, whether a gun is holstered or fired, whether a bomb is defused or detonated, whether a war is averted or fought, whether the survival of the human race is guaranteed or forfeited—*all these things are decided during the trial of the people who have wronged us.*

With so much at stake, winning this trial is of paramount importance to all people. As we've seen, our very survival depends on it. But to win such a trial, we need advice we can count on—both legal *and* spiritual advice. Indeed, to win the most important trial of our lives, *we need nothing less than the best legal and spiritual advice ever offered.*

Rest easy. It's been given to us.

And it's all right here.

Read on.

NINE

The Fourth Teaching: Nonjustice

We know now that we have only two options when we've been wronged: we can either pursue justice and try to take our happiness back from the person who wronged us, or we can pursue forgiveness and try to restore our happiness from within. We haven't discussed the benefits of pursuing forgiveness yet because we first had to understand the costs of seeking justice. We've seen that these costs are horrific. Read the newspapers. Watch the news shows on television. Count the cost of pursuing justice in your own life. After weighing all these costs, the alternative of forgiveness starts looking a whole lot more attractive.

The most important reason to forgive your enemy is to restore your own happiness. In this lifetime.

How can forgiving your enemy restore your happiness? There are three ways. First, forgiveness works the miracle of severing the past from the present and the future. The slate is wiped clean—not your enemy's slate, but *your own.* You free yourself from reliving the pain caused by the wrong you suffered and retake control over your own emotional well-being. You recognize that the wrong is safely in the past, where it belongs. This immediately relieves the pain you were experiencing, and by relieving the pain, happiness becomes possible again in the present.

Such is the miracle of forgiveness. It is a gift we either offer to or withhold from *ourselves,* not our enemies. Forgiveness enacts a very simple law taught by the great spiritual masters: If you choose to reflect upon an injury, you will experience that injury; but if you choose not to reflect upon an injury, you will not experience it. In other words, God gave us the ability to forgive not to make others happy *but to make ourselves happy.* Suffering serves only to keep us separated from each other and from God. Forgiving the wrongs that have befallen us is therefore never a sign of weakness. It is instead the holy path God created for us to achieve happiness and freedom *no matter what has happened to us in the past.* Our constant attempts to bring prior injustices kicking and screaming from the past into the present only cause us to remain unhappy. Thus, to refuse to forgive is to insist upon our own suffering—we hurt ourselves, not our enemies.

Forgiveness is the path to happiness.

The second way forgiveness restores happiness is that by forgiving your enemies, you free yourself from repeating and magnifying the wrong that caused you such pain. Remember that when you've been wronged, the resulting emotional pain and unhappiness come from the perception that you're separated and no longer loved *by the person who wronged you.* If you engage in hurtful conduct designed to take happiness from this person, not only do you reexperience your own unhappiness, but you separate yourself even farther from this person—the very person from whom you wanted respect and love. By seeking justice, you make it almost impossible to be respected and loved by this person, and almost impossible to be respected and loved by yourself. In other words, by pursuing justice, you create and perpetuate the very situation that caused you pain in the first place. On the other hand, by pursuing forgiveness, you reunite spiritually with the person who harmed you and restore your happiness *from within.*

The third way forgiveness restores happiness is that when you forgive, you acknowledge the sacred truth that you and the person who wronged you are One, and thus to hurt this person is to hurt yourself. Here, we have the highest teaching of forgiveness, taught by the great spiritual masters but so difficult for most of us to understand. Fortunately, understanding this teaching is not required to reap the benefits of forgiveness here and now. Like computers and automobiles, forgiveness works whether we understand how or not. But for those who wish to know, this teaching helps us realize that when we forgive our worst enemy, we take a step toward reunion with this person and with God. By doing so we demonstrate that there is *only God* and, therefore, we really have no enemies and the wrong we perceived was but an illusion—a mistake in our perception. Forgiveness as such becomes an act of supreme strength and sublime knowing, the sacred remembrance of our Divinity and the sacred acknowledgment that we are not our bodies. Understood thus, forgiveness becomes a demonstration that we cannot be harmed or wronged, because we are nothing less than a Child of God to whom all things have been given. Again, this is a difficult, metaphysical teaching that we need not accept or understand to experience the benefits of forgiveness.

What exactly are those benefits?

1. Restoration of our happiness *now.*
2. Elimination of the suffering *now.*

Sound good?

Sure it does. Yet despite the benefits of forgiveness, which any sane person would jump at, we continue to crave justice. Why? Because we're addicted to it. Hence the million dollar question: How can we ever break our justice addiction and make forgiveness possible?

Don't despair. Help is on the way.

The Middle Step: *Nonjustice*

The teaching of nonviolence demonstrated for us by great souls such as Mahatma Gandhi and Martin Luther King, Jr., was a powerful first step in breaking our addiction to justice and making possible the affirmative act of forgiveness. By practicing nonviolence, we learned that even if we cannot forgive our enemies—and even if we must succumb to our addiction and pursue justice against them—by abstaining from violence we can mitigate some of the most terrible costs of pursuing justice and begin to bring about peace in our world.

Nonviolence has not, however, freed us from our justice addiction. By its terms, it is incomplete, because nonviolence targets only the most wretched symptom of the underlying addiction. Like the drug methadone to a heroin addict, nonviolence to a justice addict does much to deaden the pain, but it's powerless to wipe out the addiction itself, leaving behind the merciless cravings for punishment and retribution. Even where nonviolence has been practiced faithfully, the pain of conflict and separation remains, tempting a return to violence at any moment. Although the teaching of nonviolence has done much to restore peace and happiness in our world, complete peace and happiness continue to elude us. This is because of the following principle:

Every appeal to justice serves only to magnify conflict, disunity, unhappiness, and the feeling that we are not loved.

What we need, therefore, is a form of nonviolence that targets the justice addiction itself. We need . . . *nonjustice.*

Unlike the term "injustice," which means unfairness, the term "nonjustice"—like the term nonviolence—means "abstention from" something. Because the word *nonjustice* isn't yet recognized in our dictionaries, we'll need to define it here. *Nonjustice* means, simply and powerfully, "to abstain from the pursuit of justice":

Nonjustice *is the Middle Step between nonviolence and forgiveness. Even when we are unable to forgive our enemies, we can break our justice addiction and win the most important trial of our lives by taking the less difficult Middle Step of practicing nonjustice and not further harming ourselves.*

I'm referring to nonjustice as the "Middle Step" between nonviolence and forgiveness because the affirmative act of forgiving our enemies isn't required at this stage. Our addiction to justice has proven far too strong, and the leap of faith from injury to forgiveness has proven far too great for most of us to make consistently. Rather, all that's required at this stage is to refrain from doing that which harms us. By not harming ourselves—by not pursuing justice—our happiness returns and forgiveness becomes possible and, indeed, inevitable. Thus, nonjustice is the middle step along the path toward resolving conflicts and restoring happiness. First, abstain from using violence. Second, abstain from pursuing justice. Third, experience the lasting benefits of forgiveness. Conflict gone. Happiness restored.

Nonjustice is a teaching that should appeal to us. We're actually being instructed here to do *absolutely nothing.* No grand gestures need be performed nor magical incantations uttered. No purifications, deprivations, or self-flagellations are necessary. No impossible-to-offer words of forgiveness or roses and kisses need be bestowed upon our enemies. To the contrary, we're explicitly instructed to sit back, relax, and do nothing at all. Simply observe, in the silence, how peace and happiness begin to reappear in your life because you're no longer pushing them away. Is this not a teaching anybody can follow? Is this not the teaching we've longed to hear?

Ah, you say, but doing nothing is always more difficult than it sounds. If doing nothing were so easy, then there would be no such thing as an addiction to justice—or an addiction to anything else for that matter. By definition, addictions are *compulsions to do something.* How then can we possibly abstain from pursuing justice when we're so hopelessly attracted to it? How can we consistently apply the teaching of nonjustice and be assured of winning the most important trial of our lives?

In the next two chapters, you'll find reliable, easy-to-use instructions for practicing nonjustice in any situation. In fact, you're about to be given free access to an entire Nonjustice System that can resolve any conflict in your life and restore your happiness within minutes. You'll never think about justice the same way again.

TEN

The Fifth Teaching:
The Nonjustice System

If the justice system systematizes the pursuit of justice in our world and produces suffering, then what is needed is a *nonjustice system* that systematizes the pursuit of nonjustice and produces happiness.

What would it look like?

It would look like our present justice system, but it would operate very differently.

When justice systems were first introduced in ancient times, they were a vast improvement over the uncivilized chaos and barbarism of vendetta and retaliation we then employed to resolve our disputes. Even today, when justice systems are removed from modern societies (during natural disasters or political uprisings, for example), we tend to devolve back into our ancient behaviors of violence and brutality. But we've arrived at a crossroads here in the twenty-first century. Our justice systems have long since reached their maximum usefulness and now stand in the way of peace. Rather than resolving conflicts, our justice systems instigate them. Rather than restoring happiness, our justice systems cause suffering. Rather than breaking the justice addiction, our justice systems stimulate our desire for more. We need a new system for resolving conflicts that will achieve the opposite results. As we've seen, our very survival depends on it.

To create a new system for resolving conflicts, we should start by identifying the flaws in our present systems. Even if pursuing justice were a desirable activity, our justice systems have become increasingly complex, inaccessible, inefficient, and corrupt. We see this in a variety of ways: in the disparity of judicial outcomes based upon wealth and connection; in the profound distrust of lawyers, judges, and juries; in the interference by other branches of government in what is perceived to be a runaway judiciary; in the inability of the poor to access the courts; in the search for alternative dispute resolution methods to reduce costs and speed results; in the dissatisfaction of victims and the public with outcomes even when "just" verdicts are rendered; and in escalating insurance costs and the growing discontent with our tort system. We also see this, at the farthest extreme, in the birth of the modern terrorist, who perceives no viable means of resolving disputes other than vendetta and retaliation, plunging us again into the uncivilized chaos and barbarism from which justice systems were supposed to deliver us.

If we could start all over and create the "ideal justice system," the following features would probably be on most people's wish list:

- The ideal justice system would be free and available to all

- The ideal justice system would be easy to use and not require an attorney to comprehend or negotiate

- The ideal justice system would be available everywhere, without a specific geographic courthouse or location

- The ideal justice system would be accessible whenever disputes arise, 24 hours a day, 7 days a week

- The ideal justice system would not depend upon the ability to compel opposing parties or witnesses to participate or the right to due process

- The ideal justice system would not depend upon the availability or impartiality of judges or juries

- The ideal justice system would not be vulnerable to corruption or manipulation

- The ideal justice system would provide a speedy resolution of disputes

- The ideal justice system would yield consistently fair results

Criteria for an Ideal Nonjustice System

Using this wish list as a starting point, we can develop criteria for constructing an ideal *Nonjustice System* by simply incorporating the benefits of pursuing nonjustice and forgiveness identified in chapter 9, the reasons why we're addicted to the pursuit of justice discussed in chapter 7, and the costs and benefits of pursuing justice also discussed in chapter 7. When we do this, we arrive at the following criteria for the ideal *Nonjustice System:*

- The ideal *Nonjustice System* would break the justice addiction, make forgiveness possible, and restore our happiness

- The ideal *Nonjustice System* would instantly stop the pain of being wronged and make us feel united, loved, and happy again

- The ideal *Nonjustice System* would assure us that we are not alone

- The ideal *Nonjustice System* would assure us that we have been vindicated

- The ideal *Nonjustice System* would restore our self-esteem

- The ideal *Nonjustice System* would prevent future wrongdoing

- The ideal *Nonjustice System* would produce none of the costs of pursuing justice (e.g., human suffering, personal danger, high financial costs, high social costs, risk of retaliation)

- The ideal *Nonjustice System* would make its users feel that their craving for justice has been satisfied

- The ideal *Nonjustice System* would produce a complete,

final, and meaningful resolution of disputes that brings about lasting security and peace

• The ideal *Nonjustice System* would not depend upon the threat of sanctioned violence to resolve disputes

• The ideal *Nonjustice System* would neither create nor perpetuate the desire for justice

A System for Winning the Most Important Trial of Your Life

By combining the attributes of the ideal justice system with the criteria for an ideal nonjustice system, I have created a reliable system for practicing nonjustice and winning the most important trial of your life. This system comprises the nine steps set forth in the next chapter and explained in detail below. I call it, simply but powerfully, *The Nonjustice System*.

Because we are fond of our justice systems, The Nonjustice System retains the appearance of those systems, processing our disputes in the familiar phases of indictment, trial, verdict, sentencing, appeal, and punishment. Unlike traditional justice systems, however, The Nonjustice System is an entirely self-contained process in which all proceedings that would have taken place in a courtroom can be conducted within your own home—or in your car or while walking down a sidewalk. Any person can thus safely, quickly, and easily obtain a full hearing and resolution of his or her grievances without resorting to justice or being dependent upon the actions and decisions of others—and without harming others or themselves.

As we have wished above, The Nonjustice System is free to access, available anytime and anywhere, and is so easy to use that even a child can master it. The Nonjustice System does not require an attorney, does not depend upon the ability to compel opposing parties or witnesses to participate, does not depend upon the availability or impartiality of judges and juries, does not depend upon the threat of violence to resolve disputes, and is not vulnerable to corruption and manipulation by others. Most importantly, The Nonjustice System shows us how to abstain from pursuing justice. Thus, The Nonjustice System breaks the justice addiction, restores our peace and happiness, and helps us win the most important trial of our lives.

The Nonjustice System does all this by first satisfying our craving for justice and encouraging us to try, convict, sentence, and punish the people who have wronged us—right now. No need to hire a lawyer. No need to file a lawsuit. The Nonjustice System provides everything necessary: the courtroom, the prosecutor, the defense attorney, the judge, jury, appellate court, jailer, and executioner. Our urge for justice is neither ignored nor criticized but rather acknowledged and accepted by allowing us to prosecute the case through the eight familiar steps of a judicial proceeding, but with us serving as the primary actor:

1. The Indictment—*You are the Prosecutor*
2. The Arraignment—*You are the Defendant*
3. The Trial—*You are the Witness*
4. The Summation—*You are the Defense Attorney*
5. The Verdict—*You are the Jury*
6. The Sentence—*You are the Judge*
7. The Appeal—*You are the Appellate Court*
8. The Punishment—*You are the Sheriff, Jailer, Torturer, and Executioner*

These eight steps of the traditional judicial system—the very institution we have designed to systematize retribution and punishment—are transformed into "The Nine Steps of Nonjustice" by adding one additional step, called "The Final Judgment—*You are God.*"

Don't allow this last step to frighten you. By assuming God's perspective in The Nonjustice System for just a moment, you receive deep insight into the situation and experience what it truly means to have the final authority to forgive or condemn another human being. You will see very clearly that that which you would condemn is also that which you are. In this way, you will learn the true teaching of *nonjustice* and the true power of forgiveness. In this way, your conflicts will be resolved and your happiness restored.

Proving The Nonjustice System

Many sweeping claims are being made here about The Nonjustice System. Indeed, what is claimed is nothing less than deliverance from suffering and a path to salvation itself. Jesus gave us a reliable method for testing the truth of such claims:

> Ye shall know them by their fruits. Do men gather grapes or thorns, or figs or thistles? Even so every good tree bringeth forth good fruit; but a corrupt tree bringeth forth evil fruit. A good tree cannot bring forth evil fruit, neither can a corrupt tree bring forth good fruit. Every tree that bringeth not forth good fruit is hewn down, and cast into the fire. Wherefore by their fruits ye shall know them (Matthew 7:16–20).

Like the fruit of a tree, to assess the claims made here about The Nonjustice System, you need only taste it for yourself. You are therefore invited, at this very moment, to have your day in a very different kind of court—a court of Divine Creation—and experience firsthand the difference between justice and *nonjustice.*

Think now of a person who has hurt or angered you recently, a person against whom you hold a grievance. It could be anybody: enemy, friend, or acquaintance; parent, sibling, or spouse; even God or yourself. The subject of your dispute can be anything. It might be a slight, an insult, an insensitivity, or an act of disrespect; it might be a withholding, a disloyalty, an infidelity, or a theft of something you hold precious; it might be a termination, a business dispute, or an act of harassment; it might be a physical attack, a robbery, a rape, or even a murder. Whatever the conflict, if you can think of it right now, it is still unresolved and causing you to suffer. It is, therefore, the perfect dispute to submit to The Nonjustice System for final resolution. You risk nothing by doing so. No training is required. You will be shown what to do at each step. The entire case against the person who wronged you can be heard and resolved in minutes. And afterward, if you're dissatisfied with the results, you can still go back to pursuing justice.

I encourage you to be skeptical. The Nonjustice System seeks to expose the truth about the justice systems around which we have organized ourselves for centuries, and through which we continue to justify our acts of oppression and violence. You have the right to demand that The Nonjustice System prove the claims made here. To do this, you are asked only to approach and use The Nonjustice System honestly and to follow it through to completion. If you do, the proof of these claims will become immediately manifest. You will find that your disputes with your enemies have ceased to exist, that the pain of your separation has ended, and that the craving you feel for justice has been broken. You will experience great inner peace, joy, freedom, and happiness because the power and the possibility of forgiveness will be upon you.

My friend, your endless journey through the darkness in pursuit of justice is nearly over. It was begun by Cain so very long ago, but it can be ended today with you. You no longer need lawyers, guns, or money to resolve your disputes. Everything you need is right here. The next step is up to you.

ELEVEN

The Nine Steps of Nonjustice

Welcome to The Nonjustice System.

Your case against the person who wronged you will be processed in the following nine steps:

1. The Indictment
2. The Arraignment
3. The Trial
4. The Summation
5. The Verdict
6. The Sentence
7. The Appeal
8. The Punishment
9. The Final Judgment

In each of these steps, you will be asked to provide information or answer questions. You will find the system at its most powerful if you record your responses, but this is not mandatory. Only two things are required for your disputes to be resolved and your happiness to be guaranteed. First, you must be honest about the information and answers you provide. Second, you must follow the system through to completion. Remember, you are the person who has been wronged, and you are the person who is suffering. If you mislead The Nonjustice System, you mislead yourself.

Step One

The Indictment—You Are the Prosecutor

*You are now the **prosecutor** in The Nonjustice System. Wrongs have been committed against you. Your role as prosecutor is to charge the defendant with these wrongs:*

a. Identify the defendant by name.

b. Recall the circumstances that gave rise to the offense.

c. Recall the specific conduct of the defendant that harmed you.

d. Recall the injury, pain, or damages you suffered.

e. Name the specific wrong(s) the defendant committed against you.

Step Two

The Arraignment—You Are the Defendant

*You are now the **defendant** in The Nonjustice System. You have been formally charged. Your role as the defendant is to enter your plea to the charge:*

Do you plead GUILTY and accept responsibility for committing these wrongs, or do you plead INNOCENT and demand a trial?

If you plead GUILTY, advance to Step Six.

If you plead INNOCENT, continue on to Step Three.

Step Three

The Trial—You Are the Witness

The defendant has pled innocent to the crimes as charged and demanded a trial.

*You are now a **witness** testifying at the trial of the defendant in The Nonjustice System. You are under oath. Your role as a witness is to tell the jury what happened:*

a. Recall again the circumstances that gave rise to the offense.

b. Recall again the specific conduct of the defendant that hurt you.

c. Recall again the injury, pain, or damages you suffered.

d. What, if any, additional facts would the defendant raise in his or her defense?

e. What, if any, mitigating circumstances would the defendant raise in his or her defense?

Step Four

The Summation—You Are the Defense Attorney

The evidence has been submitted and the prosecution and defense have rested the factual presentations of their cases.

*You are now the **defense attorney** representing the defendant in*

The Nonjustice System. Your role as the defense attorney is to sum-marize the defendant's case and convince the jury that the defendant is innocent:

    a. What, if any, arguments would the defendant raise in his or her defense?

    b. What, if any, excuses would the defendant raise in his or her defense?

Step Five

The Verdict—You Are the Jury

All evidence and arguments for the prosecution and defense have been presented. The trial is over.

*You are now the **jury** in The Nonjustice System. Your role as the jury is to decide whether the defendant is guilty or innocent:*

Based upon all the facts, circumstances, arguments, and excuses presented, do you find the defendant: GUILTY or INNOCENT as charged?

If you find the defendant GUILTY, proceed on to Step Six.

If you find the defendant INNOCENT, your dispute has been resolved and you may exit The Nonjustice System.

Step Six

The Sentence—You Are the Judge

The defendant has either pled guilty or been found guilty of the wrongs as charged.

*You are now the **judge** in The Nonjustice System. Your role as* *the judge is to sentence the defendant for the crimes he or she has committed:*

State the sentence as specifically as possible:

a. How exactly should the defendant be punished for these wrongs?

b. What exactly must the defendant do?

c. What specific forms of suffering must be inflicted upon the defendant?

d. How much suffering must the defendant endure? For how long?

Step Seven

The Appeal—You Are the Appellate Court

Congratulations. You have successfully tried, convicted, and sentenced the person who wronged you. But the defendant has filed an appeal, asking that your verdict and sentence be overturned before the punishment is administered.

*You are now the **appellate court** in The Nonjustice System. Your role as the appellate court is to review the verdict and sentence against the defendant:*

a. Consider again the verdict and sentence you rendered.

b. Are you certain your verdict is correct, based upon all the arguments and evidence?

c. Are you certain your sentence fits the crime?

d. Based upon your answers to the above two questions, how do you rule? Should your verdict be AFFIRMED and your sentence carried out, or should your verdict and sentence be OVERTURNED and the defendant set free?

e. If you have affirmed your verdict and sentence, proceed on to Step Eight.

f. If you have overturned your sentence, repeat Step Six and then proceed.

g. If you have overturned both the verdict and the sentence, your dispute has been resolved and you may exit The Nonjustice System.

Step Eight

The Punishment—You Are the Sheriff,
Jailer, Torturer, and Executioner

The verdict and sentence against the defendant have been affirmed. The defendant's appellate rights have been exhausted. The punishment must be administered without further delay.

*You are now the **sheriff, jailer, torturer, and executioner** in The Nonjustice System. Your role is to carry out the sentence:*

a. Imagine every detail of carrying out the sentence.

b. Imagine what the place where you are punishing the defendant looks and smells like.

c. Imagine the temperature and sounds.

d. Imagine exactly what the person who wronged you looks like as the punishment begins.

e. Imagine inflicting the punishment and how you feel doing this.

f. Imagine seeing the person who wronged you suffer in great agony, or imagine them struggling to hide the pain.

g. Imagine hearing the person who wronged you beg for mercy, or imagine them remaining stubborn and unrepentant.

h. Imagine continuing with the punishment despite the defendant's pleas, or imagine increasing the intensity of the punishment when the defendant shows no sign of remorse.

i. Imagine what the person who wronged you is feeling and thinking as the punishment continues.

j. How do *you* feel as you administer the punishment?

k. Does punishing the defendant relieve your suffering?

l. Does punishing the defendant make you happy?

m. Does punishing the defendant heal your pain?

n. Does punishing the defendant make you feel loved again?

o. Does punishing the defendant bring you inner peace?

p. Does punishing the defendant bring you joy?

q. Does punishing the defendant cause you to suffer in any new ways?

r. Have you shown mercy to the defendant?

s. Is there any room in your heart for mercy?

Step Nine

The Final Judgment—You Are God

Your wish has been granted in full. You have brought the person who wronged you to justice. You have proven that you have been hurt deeply, and now you have hurt back. Your craving for justice has been satisfied. Yet even still does your suffering continue. Justice has not brought you happiness. It has brought you only misery.

Do you wish for your suffering to end? Do you wish to feel free, happy, loved, and joyful again?

*It is in your power to do this, at this very moment, for you now have the opportunity to be as **GOD**, and God can do all things.*

*Even though you have found your brother or sister guilty, and even though you believe your punishment is just, you alone have the power to end your suffering. You can do this by ending your pursuit of justice. It is your pursuit of justice that is causing your suffering, and it is by ending your pursuit of justice that your happiness will be restored. You alone have the power to do this. **Your role as GOD in The Nonjustice System is to set yourself free:***

a. Imagine how you would feel if you exercised God's power and stopped pursuing justice against the person who wronged you.

> Would you feel relieved?
> Would you feel joyful?
> Would you feel happy?
> Would you feel loved?
> Would your suffering be ended?
> Would your pain be healed?
> Would you feel free to live your life again?

b. Imagine how the person who wronged you would feel if you exercised God's power and ended your pursuit of justice?

> Would he or she feel relieved?
> Would he or she feel joyful?
> Would he or she feel happy?
> Would he or she feel loved?
> Would his or her suffering be ended?
> Would his or her pain be healed?
> Would he or she feel free to live their life again?

c. Look again upon the person whom you would condemn.

> Do you not see, now, that this person is a Child of
> God?
>
> Do you not see, now, that this person is *YOU?*
>
> Do you not see that it is *YOUR* freedom, *YOUR*
> happiness, and *YOUR* soul that has been on
> trial here, not theirs?
>
> Do you not see that by pursuing justice against
> your brother or sister, you have been pursu-
> ing justice against *YOURSELF?*

d. You know now that there is only one way to relieve
yourself of the pain you feel. You know now that there
is only one sure course, one sure alternative, one sure
act, that can release you from your suffering.

e. Only by ending your pursuit of justice can you end
your own suffering.

f. Only by ending your pursuit of justice for the past can
you free yourself in the present and future.

g. Only by ending your pursuit of justice can you experience true happiness and joy.

h. Only by ending your pursuit of justice can you find
true peace, love, and security.

i. Only by practicing nonjustice can you offer forgiveness.

> Only by offering forgiveness can you receive for-
> giveness.
>
> Only by receiving forgiveness can you experience
> freedom and salvation.

j. *You* are a Child of God.

> A Child of God cannot be harmed or threatened.

> The belief that you have been harmed is just that, a belief.
> Like any other belief, you can choose to accept or reject it.

k. You are as *God* now. You alone have the ability to relieve your own suffering and demonstrate the power of nonjustice to yourself and the world. You alone, in this simple act of nonjustice, have the power to experience the peace and love of God.

l. Will you accept the gift of nonjustice and live in the light, or will you reject it and return to the darkness of your pain and the lie that pursuing justice against your brother or sister can bring about anything but more suffering for YOURSELF?

You are as God now.
What is your Final Judgment?
Is your pursuit of justice ENDED or will it CONTINUE?
Are you FORGIVEN or UNFORGIVEN?

TWELVE

The Benefits of Practicing Nonjustice

After you have submitted one or two disputes to The Nonjustice System, you will find that the next time you feel wronged or upset, you will process the steps of nonjustice instinctively, without even consulting this book. Very little effort will be required on your part. You will remember how good you felt when you did it the first time, and you will remember each of the steps because they are the same familiar steps of the justice system you have known most of your life. You are simply using them for a different purpose now—a holy purpose.

Yet even though you will process the steps instinctively and rapidly, your craving for justice will continue to be strong, and you will inevitably succumb to it. Do not worry, and please do not pursue justice against yourself because of this. Give yourself time. You are retraining your mind how to think and breaking a life-long addiction. That you are now thinking about practicing nonjustice in response to an injustice is enough. You are very close to ending your addiction altogether.

With a little more practice, you will find yourself skipping ahead to the final two steps of The Nonjustice System when you feel wronged. This is a sign of great progress, for in these two steps the pursuit of justice is transformed into the practice of nonjustice. You will begin to see the intensity and duration of your justice cravings being reduced. Retribution and retaliation will seem less attractive. You will probably still succumb to pursuing justice, but you will find that you end your pursuit more quickly, and you will be keenly sensitive to how badly it makes you feel. You are very close now to ridding yourself of what has caused you misery all your life. You are very close now to accomplishing what seemed impossible all your life.

Finally, with just a little more practice, you will discover that you do not need to rely upon any of the steps of The Nonjustice System. When you are wronged, your first instinct after sensing the pang of justice will be to pacify it by immediately practicing nonjustice. Holding your tongue, calming your emotions, and tempering your reaction will come easily. You will crave the peace and happiness that comes from practicing nonjustice, and you will be repulsed by the way pursuing justice makes you feel. You will have broken your justice addiction.

At this point, you will begin to experience a dramatic change in your life.

Your relationships with others will improve. You will feel less conflict and strife. You will feel more safe, peaceful, and happy. The people with whom you interact will seem more trustworthy and kind to you, and you to them. You will attract more of such people and more calm into your life. Your life will seem easier somehow, as if the weight of the world has been lifted from your shoulders.

And indeed it has.

For the world has suffered from the pursuit of justice since the beginning of time.

But for you, this suffering will be over. The long hard journey will have come to an end. And by your demonstration of the practice of nonjustice to others, it will soon come to an end for them as well. You will have given them, and yourself, the greatest gift of all—the gift of salvation and happiness.

THIRTEEN

Practicing Nonjustice vs. Preventing Injustice

The Nonjustice System can be applied to any wrong that has occurred in the past, whether it happened a moment ago or many years ago. For all such wrongs, the principle of nonjustice promises that happiness, peace, and freedom will be restored to the present if we abstain from pursuing justice and thereby refrain from harming ourselves. Nonjustice thus prevents troubles in the past from infecting the present. But this raises the question of whether, and how, the principle of nonjustice might be applied to threats of future harm and wrongdoing. What of the career criminal, the recidivist, the person who represents a danger to society? What of the person pointing a gun at you right now?

We learned earlier that the pursuit of justice is the primary motivation behind most criminal acts. This means that most career criminals are, at bottom, hard core justice addicts. Their desire for justice burns so hotly that they are willing to do anything to get it—even risk imprisonment by engaging in illegal conduct. The difference between career criminals and the career police officers and prosecutors who seek justice against them is not as great as it may seem. Both are dedicated to seeking justice, but for career criminals the pursuit of justice is entirely self-aggrandizing and knows no social bounds, whereas legitimized participants within the justice system normally operate on behalf of society itself and within agreed-upon justice-seeking limits.

Repeat offenders, and the communities victimized by them, are therefore among those who will benefit most from the teaching of nonjustice. Nonjustice helps recidivists break their justice addiction, freeing them of their craving for justice, and ending their desire to commit crimes to get it. By contrast, merely jailing these people serves only to deepen their hunger for justice and their desire to engage in further criminal conduct. Having been taught since childhood to seek justice when wronged, and having become proficient at it (albeit in very destructive ways), they feel doubly wronged when they are punished for it—triply so when, after "paying their debt to society," society rejects them, refusing to invite them back into the community with jobs, housing, and basic human support.

This makes our present justice system an incubator for career criminals—not only because it perpetuates a criminal culture within prisons but, more importantly, because the justice meted out reinforces rather than reduces antisocial justice-seeking behavior. Teaching the practice of nonjustice is the only real hope of breaking this cycle, making nonjustice an ideal tool of crime prevention.

But what about those who either ignore or do not receive the teaching of nonjustice and continue wreaking havoc upon society? Are we to stand by and do nothing, forgiving the past while knowing full well they will harm us and themselves again? Here I propose a compromise solution only slightly less unorthodox than the teaching of nonjustice itself. For such people, a period of confinement may well be necessary, but to avoid the problems just discussed, confinement must not be imposed as punishment for past crimes but rather solely as a means of protecting society, and the perpetrators themselves, from future wrongdoing. This would mean converting the criminal justice system into a "Criminal Prevention System." Imprisonment under this system would become an act of love, not retribution—a service and a gift to those so terribly lost to their justice addiction as well as to the innocent and unprotected members of society. Adjudications within the Criminal Prevention System would ask juries not only to determine the guilt or innocence of the defendant for prior criminal conduct but also to determine the *likelihood* of the defendant to engage in future criminal conduct for the sake of preventing it. This determination would be based not only upon a defendant's prior criminal history but also upon a thorough understanding of its precursors and the probabilities of repetition.

If a jury determines "beyond a reasonable doubt" that a defendant is *both* guilty of a past crime *and* that future crimes are likely, then the defendant would be incarcerated until such time as the likelihood of committing future crimes is reduced or eliminated. If a likelihood of future wrongdoing cannot be established beyond a reasonable doubt, then the defendant should be set free even if found guilty of committing a past crime because any imprisonment under such circumstances would be solely to seek justice. The period of incarceration under this new system also would be very different than it is now. Rather than being hallmarked by a punitive deprivation of dignity and freedom, intensive efforts would be made to identify the source of the defendant's antisocial justice-seeking behavior and to rectify it. The teaching and practice of nonjustice would necessarily play a large role in this aspect of the system. In this role, nonjustice would become not only a tool of crime prevention but also of criminal rehabilitation.

These proposals might seem far-fetched at first, but they're more practical than they appear and must be compared to the alternative. A defendant's likelihood of committing future crimes is already taken into account by judges during the sentencing phase of criminal prosecutions. Shifting this determination to the jury and adding it to the proof required of the prosecution during the guilt or innocence phase would not be overly burdensome or difficult. Yet the effect would be to safely and dramatically reduce the number of people in our prisons. Only those found likely to commit crimes again would receive terms of confinement. For the others, who represent little or no danger to society, social nonjustice would be practiced, freeing society and the defendant from further suffering. Perhaps these people would receive mandatory nonjustice training to help them refrain from engaging in future criminal conduct and to remind them, and ourselves, of the reason they have been freed and the forgiveness they have received.

Can any jury perfectly predict the future? No. Some

defendants thought to be of little risk will commit grievous crimes, and some who pose little risk may be unnecessarily confined. But these errors now occur with appalling regularity under our present criminal justice system, which is rife with recidivists and undertakes no effort to make this important public safety determination. By asking juries to assess future risks, and by asking prosecutors to prove them, we are finally confronting the problem.

Will we lose an important means of deterring crime if we're not punishing people who do wrong? No. First, as discussed earlier, the widespread teaching and practice of nonjustice is the best deterrent to crime because it targets the root of criminal conduct, which is the craving for justice. Second, there's still a threat of incarceration under the reforms I'm suggesting, and repeat offenders would remain in prison. Third, we need to be more honest about just how effective (or ineffective) our present system is at deterring crime. Although we've been experiencing a downward trend in criminal victimization since the 1970s, *in 2001 alone 24.2 million personal and household crimes were committed in the United States* (Bureau of Justice Statistics, September 9, 2002). That's an awful lot of crime to be proclaiming our present justice system an effective deterrent. Remember, our justice system has been around since the beginning of the nation and has had more than two hundred years, and almost limitless resources, to achieve results. As mentioned at the beginning of this book, we currently spend $167 billion each year on criminal justice, prosecuting 14 million criminal cases annually, and imprisoning 2.1 million people based solely upon what they did in the past. If this is not the very definition of a broken, far-fetched system for resolving conflicts, then I don't know what is. The human race has tread the misbegotten path of justice-seeking for thousands of years now. The time for a new approach is long overdue.

We're left, then, with the question of what, if anything, nonjustice has to say about imminent threats of harm, such as a person pointing a gun at you.

The fundamental teaching of nonjustice is that we should refrain from doing that which causes our own suffering. If inaction in the face of imminent harm will cause our suffering, then it follows that we should act. Conversely, if action in the face of imminent wrongdoing will cause our suffering, then we should refrain from action. Thus, nonjustice does not teach that we must become victims of injustice.

But beware. The question of whether action or inaction will cause suffering in a particular case is often more subtle than it seems and must be answered with a complete understanding of the situation and the consequences. The present becomes the past very quickly, and one must be alert for the moment when action to prevent a wrong not yet completed becomes punishment for a wrong already committed. The use of force in any situation invites a justice response, and many of the great spiritual masters have thus taught that the use of force, even in self-defense, causes us more suffering than being injured or even killed. Jesus not only refused to defend himself with force, but he refused to defend his family, his disciples, and his people. Mahatma Gandhi and Martin Luther King, Jr., counseled nonviolence in the face of imminent harm. George Fox taught that war can never be justified.

Nonjustice neither adds to, nor subtracts from, these teachings. It merely casts them in a slightly different light. Refrain from doing that which causes you to suffer, *but be certain first you know what causes your suffering.* The world has long pursued justice in the belief that it would relieve suffering, not produce it. We now know that this has been a deadly misunderstanding of the situation.

FOURTEEN

Practicing Nonjustice vs. Rectifying Injustice

Does nonjustice bar us from seeking material relief from past injustices? Can the victims of drunk drivers, dishonest merchants, discriminatory employers, negligent physicians, abusive spouses, and other wrongdoers do anything to restore their material well-being without risking their emotional and spiritual happiness?

As a lawyer who now practices what I call "nonjustice law," I've grappled with these questions almost daily—in my own life and in the lives of my clients.

Nonjustice teaches that whenever we seek justice—that is, whenever we attempt to restore our happiness by hurting the person who wronged us—we invariably cause ourselves to suffer. Thus, nonjustice says we shouldn't repay injustice with justice. Better to do nothing at all. If, of course, we want to be happy. That isn't always the case. We're often more than willing to sacrifice our happiness to achieve short term material gains, such as winning an argument with a fist or a money judgment with a lawsuit. Only after the victory is secured do we realize that surrendering our peace and happiness to get it was too high a price to pay; for peace and happiness were, after all, what we were hoping to achieve in the first place. As stated earlier, "Every appeal to justice serves only to magnify conflict, disunity, unhappiness, and the feeling that you are not loved."

This doesn't mean, however, that we can't ask the person who wronged us to make things right. Are we not taught to ask our Father in heaven for help, and to know our prayers are always answered?

When a material wrong has been committed, or a material mistake has been made, and we're injured as a result, we can inform the person who injured us that we're hurting, and that we need their assistance to be well again. We don't need to label this person guilty and demand retribution; nor must we try to inflict suffering upon this person in any way. We seek only to be well, and for happiness to be multiplied rather than diminished. We've practiced nonjustice to restore our emotional and spiritual happiness, and now we're appealing for help in restoring our material happiness too. In doing so, we're not only seeking help for ourselves, but we're also offering assistance to the person who wronged us. Few people in this world truly enjoy making others suffer; even the most callous among us feel intensely guilty, if only deep inside. They wish to be relieved of this guilt and to make amends but often don't know how. We can make this possible by inviting them to help us recover without judging them or seeking their own suffering. By gently asking for help, and by assuring them that we're not seeking justice, we're healing them at the same time we're healing ourselves.

In my nonjustice law practice, for example, I contact the opposing side in a very nonconfrontational manner, explaining my client's grievance but also explaining my nonjustice philosophy, sending them a copy of this book, and inviting them to visit the Nonjustice Foundation web site (www.nonjustice.org) for more information. I tell them that my client wishes to practice nonjustice and resolve the dispute amicably. More often than not, this approach disarms the other side instantly, creating a safe, nonthreatening atmosphere in which to discuss the conflict and find a mutually acceptable compromise. Most people (lawyers and clients alike) respond better to olive branches than thorns.

Nonjustice therefore does not bar us from asking for help. It does, however, teach that we forfeit our happiness if we attempt to *force* somebody to help us. In other words, after we've asked, we must not resort to justice if we don't like the answer. We may ask again, persistently but kindly, as we do in our prayers. But we don't sue God when we don't get the response we want. Neither should we sue each other. In truth, there's no difference between the two, for through whom can God possibly act other than the people around us, including the person who's harmed us? If after asking properly and persistently we don't receive the answer we want from the person who's wronged us, then perhaps what we want is not what we really need, or perhaps what we want and need will come from somebody else. Remember, God is the one who gives us life and the world around us, and God is also the one who makes possible the satisfaction of our wants and needs. God is not limited in doing so through the people we expect. Material assistance can come from anywhere the universe sees fit. Our stubborn insistence that it come from the person who wronged us is to seek justice against this person and guarantee our unhappiness.

The saying that time heals all wounds is both true and false. In my experience as a lawyer, I've observed that time seems at first to exacerbate wounds rather than heal them. It has this effect when amends aren't made within the time we expect them. If the person who has harmed us doesn't act to correct the error when we believe they should, our outrage and anger intensify, as does our craving for justice. We believe we've given the person who wronged us a reasonable amount of time to fix the problem, and now this person is multiplying the wrong by failing to act within that time. We believe our injury is being ignored and the other person is uncaring, recalcitrant, and needs to be taught a lesson. This is all a matter of perception. From the other person's perspective, he believes he's acting as reasonably as circumstances require. Patience and understanding are therefore critical in resolving disputes. I've observed that many lawsuits are filed not because the defendant believes he or she has no obligation to make amends, but because the plaintiff perceives that the defendant is shirking his or her responsibility by not acting quickly enough in making them.

In the long run, of course, time heals even the wounds it seems at first to exacerbate. Pain and memories fade away. Given enough time, most wounds are forgotten, or if not forgotten then seen as not worth fighting over any longer. In effect, time is an instrument of nonjustice, slowly and inexorably wearing down the craving for justice and making forgiveness possible. The miracle of the nonjustice teaching in this book is that it collapses time, making it possible to forgive and forget much more quickly than can be accomplished with the ordinary passage of time. A wound that might fester and cause pain for years can be healed within minutes, or even seconds, by practicing nonjustice. By contrast, seeking justice has the opposite effect, *increasing* the time that must pass before a wound can be healed and forgotten by delaying the possibility of forgiveness. But the passage of time holds no favorites. After years of fighting, most litigants (and warriors) eventually begin to wonder what they were fighting about and whether it's really worth it to continue. This is why the statistical likelihood of settling a case without a trial increases over time.

My point here is that asking for material help from the person who wronged you isn't inconsistent with the teaching of nonjustice. *And by asking rather than suing, you are no less likely to get what you want.* Remember, there's no guarantee you'll win a lawsuit. For every lawsuit that goes to trial, there's a loser, and the overall odds of "winning" are at best fifty percent. Ask any lawyer. The number of cases that should have been won but were lost roughly equals the number of cases that should have been lost but were won. There are simply too many variables; too many opportunities for error, misunderstanding, miscalculation, bias, and prejudice. Connections, emotions, and politics come into play. Sometimes, the style of your attorney's hair or the tone of her voice can make all the difference. Litigation is like rolling dice, except the dice hang spinning in the air for years before the weak gravity of the justice system finally forces them to hit the table and reveal their number. Because of this, more than ninety percent of all lawsuits end in a negotiated settlement, not a trial, where both parties have compromised significantly from their original positions. Even in the cases that do end with a verdict, only rarely do the parties accomplish what they hoped to achieve when they started. Judges and juries do the compromising for them.

What all this means is that most lawsuits end exactly the way a nonjustice request begins: by the plaintiff asking for help and the defendant granting the request in some form of compromise. The benefit of practicing nonjustice is that you can restore your peace and happiness instantly and spare yourself the time and expense of litigation, which keeps peace and happiness beyond your reach. Of course, like a lawsuit, you aren't guaranteed to get the material help you want by making a nonjustice request. Indeed, if you don't get it, you risk opening the wound and craving justice again. Thus, you must be careful not to condition your happiness on an act of capitulation. It doesn't work that way. If you're unable to accept a negative response to your request without appealing to justice, then you probably shouldn't even ask. But if you can accept such a response without pursuing justice, then, unlike litigation, you're guaranteed to get exactly what you need when you need it. In that case, your request becomes as holy as a prayer, and it's treated as such by the universe, which answers all prayers without fail. True, attempting to resolve your disputes in this way requires a certain amount of faith. Yet, when viewed honestly, attempting to resolve your disputes through litigation requires just as much faith, if not a whole lot more. The question is whether you're better off by placing your faith in God or in the justice system.

FIFTEEN

Personal Nonjustice: The Other Most Important Trial of Your Life

The principle of nonjustice applies not only to our relationships with others but also to our relationship with ourselves.

Those who have ample room in their hearts to forgive the wrongs of other people often find it next to impossible to forgive the wrongs they commit themselves. We may see personal forgiveness as the ultimate act of arrogance because we know ourselves far too well and our misdeeds in far too much detail. With somebody else, we might be asked to forgive a single instance of wrongdoing, but with ourselves there may be decades of bad acts to forgive. We're not only convinced that this is impossible but that we wouldn't deserve forgiveness even if it were. From childhood, many of us are taught to believe we're flawed, reprehensible, unlovable, and unforgivable. We're taught to believe that if we forgive ourselves, if we love ourselves, if we dare to see ourselves as blessed, then we've committed the greatest of all sins because we've equated ourselves with God—even though we believe God is perfect and only capable of creating perfection.

The result of all this is that we pursue justice against ourselves with single-minded devotion and cruelty. Like a trained assassin, we become very efficient because we know every vulnerability. Our suffering is squared in the process. We're not only the victims of our relentless pursuit of justice; we're also the perpetrators of it, trapped in a vicious cycle of punishing ourselves and then punishing ourselves for punishing ourselves. We rarely feel truly happy, peaceful, united, and loved. When we do, we punish ourselves for it. When we don't, we punish ourselves for that too. There's no winning for us; there's no relief. We're determined to make ourselves the last person on earth who receives our mercy. The costs of pursuing justice against others are only a fraction of what we would make ourselves pay.

This is why the "other" most important trial in your life is the trial of *yourself.*

Like the trial of the people who've wronged us, the outcome of the trial against ourselves will determine our peace and happiness, and the peace and happiness of our families, nations, and world. Whether relationships are nurtured or destroyed, whether children are loved or abused, whether diplomas are conferred or denied, whether jobs are found or lost, whether automobile accidents are avoided or attracted, whether illness is prevented or induced, whether discrimination is conquered or encouraged, whether property is protected or stolen, whether a punch is withheld or thrown, whether a gun is holstered or fired, whether a bomb is defused or detonated, whether a war is averted or fought, whether the survival of the human race is guaranteed or forfeited—all these things are also decided during the trial of ourselves.

I'm speaking here from personal experience because I've been this way much of my life. I've treated myself very harshly. No wrong I've committed has been too small to go unpunished. I've felt guilty whenever I've felt truly good about myself. I've worried that if I ever forgave myself, I'd never improve. I lost the trial of myself over and over again, pursuing justice against myself for every wrong and suffering immensely as a result. It hurt my family, my work, my health, and my happiness.

When I came upon the teaching of The Nonjustice System, I didn't feel I could pass it on to others in good conscience until I'd experienced it for myself. I wanted to see whether the claims were true and, as Jesus said, "know them by their fruits." So I was the first person to submit a dispute to The Nonjustice System. But I was also the first person to be put on trial there. I could think of no greater villain in my life than me.

Conducting this experiment in self-justice and self-nonjustice is one of the single most important things I have done in my life. I broke my addiction to punishing myself and realized that I was, after all, worthy of forgiveness and love. I found deep wells of unspeakable peace, happiness, and joy. My relationships with my family, friends, and colleagues improved immediately. I felt more energetic because I was no longer using energy to punish myself. I thought more clearly, because my mind was no longer occupied with finding new ways to rebuke itself. I received the insight, strength, and courage to conceive of and write this book, which demonstrates the true necessity, and power, of practicing nonjustice on yourself.

I wish these things for you too.

SIXTEEN

The Nonjustice of Oneness

I have one final teaching to share with you. It may be the most precious of all.

In chapter 9 of this book, I said that the great spiritual masters have taught that the highest teaching about forgiveness is this: "When you forgive, you acknowledge the sacred truth that you and the person who wronged you are One, and thus to hurt this person is to hurt yourself."

I have always found this teaching extremely difficult to accept. How can the person who wronged me also be me? We have different bodies. We were born on different dates in different places, and we'll probably die on different dates in different places. We think different thoughts and do different things. We live different lives. How can there possibly be only One person when there are more than six billion people on this planet?

I struggled without success for many years to understand this teaching. Then one morning I sat down in the quiet and asked God to please explain it to me. Here is what I got:

Picture in your mind a clear drinking glass half filled with soap water. Now, cover the glass with your hand, shake it gently, uncover it, and look down through the opening.

You will see hundreds of soap bubbles.

These soap bubbles appear before you in all shapes and sizes: small and large, thin and fat, colored and pale, shiny and dull, opaque and translucent, together and alone, running and resting, rising and falling. New bubbles appear and old bubbles disappear. Some bubbles last only seconds while others linger many minutes. Some bubbles divide into smaller bubbles while others consume smaller bubbles to become larger bubbles.

Looking down through the top of the glass, you see that this world of soap bubbles is a very active place. It is a place of great beauty, but also a place of great danger, a place of creation and destruction, of generation and consumption, of union and separation, of attack and defense, of survival of the fittest, and of life and death.

The world of soap bubbles can be a terrifying place for a soap bubble.

But if instead of looking down through the opening, you raise the glass before your eyes and look through the side instead, you will see a very different kind of place. From this perspective, you see that all these soap bubbles are floating upon the surface of a deep, calm body of water. They are supported by this body of water and connected to it. Indeed, they are this body of water. You see now that the bubbles are simply extensions of the water itself, thin films of water arching up from its surface. The bubbles emerge from the water and return to it. Even as some of the bubbles rise and appear to float away, they never lose their connection with the water because they are simply that, water, and this they will always be.

Looking down again through the top of the glass, all these hundreds of soap bubbles appear to be independent beings with busy lives of their own. But looking through the side of the glass, you see that they are all One being with One life. They are all water. They are neither created nor destroyed, neither generated nor consumed, neither united nor divided.

Like you, the soap bubbles are free to view themselves in any way they wish, from either the top of the glass or the side. They may choose to see illusions or truth. Yet even when the soap bubbles stubbornly insist upon viewing themselves through the top of the glass, where they appear to be in constant conflict and struggling to survive, the truth of the soap bubbles remains forever secure and unchanged. The soap bubbles are, and always will be, water, sometimes extending itself and sometimes not. And just beneath the bubbles, there is now and always will be Oneness. This Oneness is the realm of the Absolute for soap bubbles, where there are no opposites and not even illusions of separation from the water are possible.

The truth is always available to the soap bubbles, if they will only choose to shift their perspective and see it—if they will only consider the possibility that their perception from the top of the glass may be inaccurate and incomplete.

The wisest soap bubbles know the truth about themselves and are not deceived by changing perspectives. They have seen their world from the side of the glass. They have seen the water that is their Source, and they have realized that they are that which created them. They know that they have nothing to fear because they know that they are not bubbles at all. They are water. They are One.

Knowing this, the wisest soap bubbles never pursue justice against other bubbles, not even against the meanest bubbles of all.

It would make no sense for them to do so.

For they would only be pursuing justice against themselves.

This is the nonjustice of Oneness.

Choose now and always to experience this Oneness.

Choose now and always to view yourself through the side of the glass.

For by doing so, you will find the Peace of God.

Questions and Answers about Nonjustice

Since writing this book, I have been asked many questions about the implications of nonjustice and its application to specific situations. I've tried to answer some of those questions here.

Are you saying the entire justice system should be scrapped?

No, I am saying the entire justice system should be reformed. The reform I am advocating is akin to the reform advocated for the Christian Church during the protestant reformation. Martin Luther, a priest himself, spoke out against the abuses of the Church, arguing that the Church was systematically separating people from God, rather than uniting them with God. Similarly, I am speaking out against the abuses of the justice system, which is systematically separating people from one another, rather than uniting them with one another. Luther argued that human beings do not require sacraments or clerics to mediate their relationship with God and bring about salvation. Similarly, I am arguing that we do not need lawsuits or attorneys to mediate our relationships with each other and bring about happiness. Luther did not advocate doing away with the Christian Church; nor do I recommend doing away with the justice system. As the protestant reformation encouraged people to accept personal responsibility for their relationships with God and their own salvation, so too am I encouraging people to accept personal responsibility for their relationships with each other and their own happiness.

Are you saying there is no role for attorneys in conflict resolution?

No. As Gandhi said, "the true function of a lawyer [is] to unite parties riven asunder." Many attorneys today fulfill this function admirably, but many do not. Attorneys are taught in law school to represent their clients zealously, which is often interpreted in practice as winning at all costs and destroying your opponent. Clients and society contribute to this problem, valuing aggressive lawyers who do battle over those who resolve problems by compromise. The most recent and egregious example of this, perhaps setting an all-time low in the history of the legal profession, is the revelation that high-ranking lawyers within the administration of President George W. Bush succumbed to the political desire for justice in the wake of the terrorist attacks of September 11, 2001, by rendering legal opinions supporting the president's suspension of the Geneva Conventions against the abuse of prisoners and sanctioning the use of torture. Those legal opinions have led to the torture and murder of prisoners in American military jails and, in turn, to the torture and murder of Americans (by the countrymen of the abused prisoners seeking justice). These lawyers have turned Gandhi's teaching on its head, making "the true function of a lawyer" in modern society into that of a cold-blooded mercenary.

What I am saying is that the role of the attorney—in the mind of both the legal profession and the public—must be changed from that of mercenary to that of peacemaker. When somebody declares in the middle of a fight, "You'll be hearing from my lawyer," this should be taken as a universal signal that peace is sought, not war. People will often need help in resolving their disputes, and lawyers have much to offer in this regard. But lawyers should adopt the physician's oath and avow, "First, do no harm." This means, at minimum, assisting clients in practicing nonjustice and restoring their happiness before reflexively sending a demand letter or filing a lawsuit or a counterclaim. As the recent mind/body/spirit movement in medicine has shown that outcomes improve when physicians take into account the whole patient—mind, body, and spirit—so I am arguing that outcomes improve when attorneys take into account the whole client—mind, body, and spirit. Winning a financial award at the expense of destroying a client's emotional and spiritual well-being cannot be considered a victory by any measure.

What about people like Adolph Hitler, Osama Bin Laden, and Saddam Hussein? Should we not seek justice against them?

No, we should not seek justice against tyrants and terrorists . . . if we want to restore our happiness. Extreme cases like these cry out the most for nonjustice. In the wake of the profound suffering such people inflict, happiness cannot possibly be restored by reliving the suffering over and over again and inflicting even more upon ourselves, the perpetrators, and innocent bystanders by seeking justice. Peace and happiness are not commodities that can be taken from a tyrant or terrorist and enjoyed by his victims. Peace and happiness come from within, not without. To find them, one must go beyond the suffering, first by practicing nonjustice and then, ultimately, by offering forgiveness as a mercy to oneself, not the tyrant. Seeking justice cannot restore happiness. It can only guarantee more unhappiness.

There is another reason not to seek justice against tyrants and terrorists. Remember that these men commit their horrific crimes *because they are convinced every step of the way that they are only seeking justice.* Hitler was convinced that exterminating the Jews was "the final solution" to injustices perpetrated by the Jews and necessary to secure Germany's "master race"; Bin Laden was convinced that destroying the World Trade Center towers was only justice for injustices perpetrated by the United States in the Islamic world; and Saddam Hussein was convinced that gassing the Kurds and torturing those who opposed him were acts of justice to ensure his personal and political survival. Tyrants and terrorists are the hardest of hard core justice addicts. To seek justice against them is merely to reinforce and reward their logic—and to encourage others to indulge their own justice cravings in ever more terrible ways. In other words, to seek justice against a tyrant or terrorist is to create more tyrants and terrorists because we are validating their motivation for committing their atrocities. This cycle has been repeated for thousands of years and will not stop until we stop seeking justice against each other.

This does not mean, of course, that we must submit willingly to butchers. We should strive to protect those at risk and oppose those who would harm them. But this can be accomplished without seeking justice for past wrongs. And, as Gandhi and others have proved, it can be done without using violence. Chapter 13 discusses this in greater detail.

Thoughtful people will always debate whether Hitler could have been stopped without violence. The assumption is that he could not, but we will never know for certain. We do know, however, that Saddam Hussein was effectively stopped from developing weapons of mass destruction and threatening his neighbors with nonviolent United Nations sanctions long before the United States attacked Iraq. Hussein had been greatly weakened and his reign was drawing to a close. We know also that the Soviet Union and the communist countries of eastern Europe were pacified without warfare. We know too that apartheid in South Africa was ended without warfare, and that the British withdrew from India in the same way. I highly recommend Jonathan Schell's *The Unconquerable World* to those searching for more examples of successful nonviolence.

Now, consider for a moment the alternative. In our own time, a small band of less than thirty Islamic extremists succeeded in killing more than 3,000 people in the United States on September 11, 2001. This was a terrible crime and a terrible loss. In response, our country insisted upon bringing the terrorists to justice—by waging wars in Afghanistan and Iraq. As of this writing, approximately 1,500 United States soldiers have been killed in these wars; 10,000 United States soldiers have been wounded; 100,000 Iraqis have been killed; 5,000 Afghans have been killed; hundreds of Iraqis, Afghans, and others have been brutally tortured at Abu Ghraib and Guantanamo Bay; and the United States has spent more than $100 billion—all in the pursuit of justice for the past crimes of September 11, 2001. Are these "just" wars? Absolutely. But don't you see? *All wars are just . . . because all wars are waged in the pursuit of justice.* That's the problem. Debating whether a war is just is a debate without meaning. The question is not whether these wars are just but whether just wars can possibly restore happiness after a terrorist attack. The answer, unequivocally, is *no.* It can only compound our suffering, as this sad example illustrates.

This does not mean happiness will never be restored to those who wage war. To the contrary, our indomitable world has recovered from all the wars ever fought. How? Because after the killing finally stops, the combatants learn again how to practice nonjustice and forgive each other. The Americans and British forgave each other after the Revolutionary War. The North and South forgave each other after the Civil War. Most of the nations of the world have forgiven each other since World War II. The United States and Vietnam have forgiven each other. And some day the United States, Iraq, Afghanistan, and Islamic extremists will forgive each other. An enemy may sometimes be defeated militarily, *but the conflict between peoples does not end until nonjustice and forgiveness are practiced.* This means that nonjustice and forgiveness are the end game of every war and raises an important question: Why bother fighting the war in the first place? Doing so merely prolongs the time until nonjustice and forgiveness are practiced and happiness is restored. We can skip all the suffering and go straight to happiness if we choose—by simply abstaining from the pursuit of justice. This principle applies not only to warfare between countries but to disputes between individuals. Conflicts and suffering end only when nonjustice and forgiveness are practiced. Why delay what is inevitable—and what we really want in the first place?

Why should victims of defective products, corporate malfeasance, medical malpractice, and institutional abuses (such as child molestation by teachers, caregivers, or priests) not seek justice in the tort system? What about the deterrent effect of tort lawsuits?

Seriously injured people such as these should not seek justice in the tort system because doing so will only prolong their suffering and prevent the restoration of their happiness. As we have seen, justice for the past always comes at the expense of peace and happiness in the present, regardless of the type or severity of the wrong perpetrated. Practicing nonjustice, and submitting these grievances to The Nonjustice System for resolution, are the only certain ways of restoring happiness *now*. This does not mean that seriously injured people cannot seek material assistance to recover from their injuries—either from the perpetrators themselves, insurance carriers, the government, or other sources. Chapter 14 contains a more thorough explanation of how to do this and why. Lawyers can be helpful in this regard and should be consulted to be certain of one's rights and the consequences of one's actions.

As for the deterrent effect of tort lawsuits, one must ask whether tortious behavior is actually encouraged by these lawsuits and, to the extent deterrence is effected, at what cost, and whether other means of deterrence are available? Starting with the costs, the lawyers who prosecute and defend these lawsuits become enriched but at the expense of innocent consumers, their own clients, and society. Society is taxed with the costs of putting on the spectacle and the insatiable demand for justice generated when multimillion dollar verdicts are announced—creating a powerful incentive for the rest of us to seek justice whenever we feel wronged. If the lawsuit is ultimately "successful," a person, company, or institution that might have been engaged in other socially beneficial activities is severely damaged or destroyed. For example, is it really in our interest to bankrupt a pharmaceutical company because it wrongfully sold a defective drug that killed thousands, when that company also manufactures drugs that save millions—and while knowing full well that money judgments cannot restore the lives of the people lost? Is it really in our interest to force Catholic dioceses that feed the hungry and house the homeless to sell their properties and pay millions of dollars to adults who were molested decades ago by depraved priests—while knowing full well that this money cannot restore their innocence or their happiness? Is it really in our interest to pay millions of dollars more every day for health care and other products and services *just so injured people can indulge their justice addictions by filing lawsuits?*

Don't get me wrong. Individuals, companies, and institutions that harm people need to be stopped from doing so again. And they need to help the people they have harmed.

Insurance pools can be made more readily accessible to accomplish the latter, without the rancor of seeking justice. For example, every day in our country, homes and businesses are destroyed and lives are disrupted or lost due to "acts of God" such as fires, floods, and storms. Yet, we do not file lawsuits against God, raging rivers, or storm systems. We file insurance claims and turn to our families, neighbors, and governments for help in getting our lives back together. Can we not do the same when a calamity is caused by a defective product, dishonest corporation, negligent physician, or abusive institution? Of course we can, but we are not satisfied with mere *help* in that case. We crave *justice*. The big money won in tort lawsuits is rarely in compensatory damages for injured people. The big money is more often in punitive damages, and damages for pain and suffering, all of which are in the nature of justice-seeking, not assistance.

The current problem in our tort system is akin to the problem in our criminal justice system, discussed in chapter 13. Both systems have become obsessively and abusively focused on justice-seeking. Any serious consideration of tort reform must therefore begin with the recognition that individuals, companies, and institutions that culpably harm people often do so for the same reasons that terrorists blow up airplanes and criminals commit crimes. They are seeking justice—whether it be justice in the form of increasing profits, fending off competition, selling more products and services, increasing stock prices, or avoiding tort lawsuits. For example, a company that has invested billions of dollars in the development, manufacturing, and marketing of a product, and that depends upon this product for much of its revenue, feels that it is unfair to be forced to withdraw the product from the market for quality or safety concerns. The company believes it is being wronged by the marketplace, the legal system, and perhaps its own customers who are misusing the product. Justice demands that the company continue to sell the product, even if thousands of people are injured. Likewise, justice demands that an institution like the Roman Catholic Church conceal the sexual abuse of children perpetrated by some of its priests. Such scandalous revelations are highly damaging to an institution that prides itself on protecting the innocent and that depends upon its reputation for doing so. Similarly, it is justice that demands that some physicians not give their patients the highest quality of care—perhaps because reimbursement rates are too low, or because the patient has been disrespectful, or because the physician is overworked.

Of course, there are also individuals, companies, and institutions that simply make honest mistakes that wind up hurting people. But regardless of the level of culpability underlying tortious conduct, seeking justice against tortfeasors has the same negative consequences as seeking justice against criminals—namely, that it encourages everybody to continue to believe the path to happiness is to seek justice against each other when we feel unhappy. In other words, seeking justice actually increases tortious behavior. Every tort lawsuit serves as a reminder that we are a justice-addicted society and that to survive in this society one must be constantly seeking justice for oneself. By contrast, the widespread teaching and practice of nonjustice is the best deterrent to tortious conduct because it targets the source of that conduct.

But what about a physician who injures patients repeatedly, or a company that continues to sell defective products, or an institution that continues to abuse those under its care? Are we to stand by and do nothing, knowing full well they will harm us again?

Here, I offer a compromise solution similar to the one I offered in chapter 13 to reform the criminal justice system. Legal action against such tortfeasors may well be necessary, but to avoid the problems of seeking justice, such action must not be pursued to redress past wrongs but rather strictly as a means of preventing future injury. This would mean converting the tort system into a "Tort Prevention System." Lawsuits under this system would ask judges and juries not only to determine liability for prior conduct but also to determine the *likelihood* of a defendant to repeat that conduct, and then to enter orders enjoining such behavior (for example, withdrawing the license of an incompetent physician, prohibiting sales of a harmful product, or creating systems to prevent and report the abuse of children). Under the Tort Prevention System, seeking punitive money judgments for past wrongs would not be permitted. Instead, nonjustice would be practiced to the benefit of all society (rather than money judgments to reward only a few), reducing court congestion, insurance premiums, products and services prices, and overall social bitterness and suffering.

This type of policing is normally left to governments, not private citizens, but many statutes today—such as civil rights, housing, and employment discrimination laws—create private rights of action, encouraging individuals to sue to prevent future wrongdoing, and awarding attorney's fees to the successful parties. There is no reason why this same concept cannot be extended to the tort system, keeping the best that it has to offer and doing away with the rest. But all such lawsuits must be handled carefully. As discussed in chapter 13, the present becomes the past very quickly, and one must be alert for the moment when a lawsuit to prevent a wrong not yet completed becomes a lawsuit seeking justice for a wrong already committed.

One final point. The power of tort lawsuits to deter tortious conduct under the current system rarely comes from the lawsuit itself. Most successful individuals, companies, and institutions can afford to pay even large money judgments as a cost of doing business. What they cannot afford is the bad publicity generated by being publicly accused of harming consumers or the public. This threatens their reputations, stock prices, and their ability to sell products and services *in the future.* It is this type of indirect pressure that prevents repeated misconduct. The forward-looking reforms I am suggesting would preserve this pressure while enabling tort lawsuits to prevent future harm much more directly and effectively and avoiding the vices of the backward-looking system we currently have. Lawyers would still have much work to do, but it would be work to benefit all of society, not to enrich only a few.

What about lawsuits seeking social justice, such as ending discrimination, stopping pollution, and protecting civil rights?

Nonjustice counters our addiction to pursuing "justice" as a synonym for revenge, retribution, payback, and vengeance. Social justice, on the other hand, evokes the opposite meaning of "justice," discussed in chapter 6, which is synonymous with fundamental fairness, equity, righteousness, and the notion that *all* people must be treated with dignity and respect, without winners or losers and without regard to what has happened in the past. This is the highest and truest form of justice, and it is to be encouraged.

Lawsuits seeking to bring about social justice by preventing injustices from happening *in the future* (as opposed to punishing injustices of the past) would not run afoul of the teaching of nonjustice. This is where lawyers have always been of great value to society. Skillful lawyers can often help prevent injustices from continuing or even happening in the first place, mitigating or eliminating conflicts before they arise. There are many examples of lawsuits that have created, maintained, or restored social justice and happiness prospectively, such as the famous case of *Brown v. Board of Education*, which outlawed racial segregation in schools. Lawsuits seeking injunctions against pollution, to improve prison conditions, and to ensure civil liberties—without seeking punishment for prior transgressions—also fall into this category.

What about serial murderers and rapists?

This question is answered at length in chapter 13.

What about small claims? What should I do if somebody breaks my window or breaches a contract?

Seeking justice for minor wrongs and inconveniences is as damaging as seeking justice for serious injuries and crimes. By seeking justice, you prolong your own suffering and postpone the restoration of your happiness. So, what do you do?

First, submit your grievance to The Nonjustice System for immediate resolution. You have nothing to lose and everything to gain. It is important to quench your justice cravings as quickly as possible.

Second, if after doing this you strongly believe you need material assistance to be made whole again, you can ask for help from the person who wronged you, as described in chapter 14. You might even want to send this person a copy of this book, invite them to visit the Nonjustice Foundation web site (www.nonjustice.org), and join you in practicing nonjustice to amicably resolve the dispute.

If you are still not satisfied after taking these measures, you have a decision to make. You can either continue to practice nonjustice and walk away with your happiness, or you can begin to pursue justice by filing suit in a small claims court. If you choose to file suit, you will again experience suffering and unhappiness. Small claims courts try to minimize this by allowing people to air their grievances quickly and informally, usually without lawyers being present. Even so, I can guarantee that you will feel very tense, angry, and unhappy when you walk into court to get justice. Is this not a powerful warning that seeking justice really does cause human suffering? You are also likely to leave feeling the same way. You will either win, lose, or your claim will be compromised. Losing and compromise carry obvious emotional consequences, but even if you win, the sensation of vindication and satisfaction will wear off and feelings of unhappiness will soon return.

The teachings in this book demonstrate that pursuing justice causes suffering. They also offer an effective way to avoid this suffering and restore happiness. But you are always free to choose to suffer in favor of pursuing justice to achieve material gains. Before you do, however, consider the rewards of practicing nonjustice and not pressing your claim. There are two. First, you will restore your happiness immediately—not in days, months, or years but *right now.*

Second, by doing this you will invite the universe (or God, serendipity, or whatever force you like) to respond to your gesture in kind by fulfilling your material wants and needs because you will have eliminated hatred, fear, and suffering from your life. You may not succeed in forcing the person who broke your window to pay for the repair, but the money to do so will come from some other source—without you forfeiting your happiness to get it. Does it really matter where the money to fix the window comes from? Must it come only from the person who broke it? Why? To teach him a lesson? To hold him accountable? Perhaps, but this is not your job in life. Your job is to make yourself happy and reunite with people, not make yourself suffer and separate yourself from others and teach them a lesson. Suing somebody will make you feel miserable. Practicing nonjustice and forgiving them will make you feel wonderful. Why deliberately choose misery? You don't know how much time you have on this planet. Better to spend it in a constant state of bliss.

What about child custody disputes?

A parent who seeks to deny a former spouse custody or visitation rights to punish the former spouse for prior transgressions is seeking justice. This parent will succeed only in inflicting further suffering upon themselves and the child, while preventing any hope of restoring happiness. Practicing nonjustice—by not opposing custody or visitation for the former spouse—is the only way out for this parent. Similarly, practicing nonjustice—by not retaliating while calmly pressing for custody or visitation—is the only way out for the former spouse who is injured by this conduct.

On the other hand, honest child custody disputes, where both parents seek custody in good faith and without any motive to inflict harm upon each other—or where one parent honestly believes the other parent will do harm to the child—are a different matter. In these cases, somebody must decide between competing viewpoints, and that somebody is the judge. This is not about justice, it is about what is in the best interest of the child *in the future.* Nonjustice is not implicated. Both parties can offer their reasons for why the decision should be made one way or the other. However, when the judge decides, the craving for justice may emerge with a vengeance. A parent who loses custody or visitation may feel hurt and want justice. Here, it becomes vital for this parent to submit the conflict to The Nonjustice System for immediate resolution. Only by practicing nonjustice can the injured parent restore his or her happiness—and help the child.

What should I do if I have been sued?

If you have been sued by somebody, your first step should be to consult with an attorney to be certain you understand your rights, obligations, and the time within which you must respond. Once these matters are out of the way, you can then turn to resolving the conflict and restoring your happiness. As a first step toward doing this, you should consider very carefully why you have been sued, *from the plaintiff's point of view, not your own,* and whether you should try to make amends. Most people do not file lawsuits lightly. They honestly believe they have been wronged and that the defendant should do something to make them feel better again. Whether their allegations are true or false, they are seeking justice. Helping them to feel better by making amends if possible will end the litigation and restore happiness for everyone. Fighting will only prolong the suffering.

If after careful consideration you feel the claims in the lawsuit are unjust and that you cannot compromise in any way, you should submit the conflict to the Nonjustice System for immediate resolution. This will help you resist the urge to seek justice against the person who sued you and thereby help you avoid multiplying your suffering. After you have done this, you should consider ways to encourage the person who sued you to submit their side of the dispute to the Nonjustice System as well. You might send them a copy of this book or invite them to visit the Nonjustice Foundation web site (www.nonjustice.org). You might tell them you are practicing nonjustice yourself and wish to resolve the dispute amicably so that happiness can be restored to all. These overtures can also be accomplished through your attorney. You may want to share this book with him or her and request that their representation be handled in a nonjustice manner. As mentioned in chapter 14, I have successfully resolved disputes for my own clients in this way. Such a peaceful approach tends to disarm the other side and create a safe, nonthreatening atmosphere in which to discuss the conflict and find a mutually acceptable compromise. Again, most people (lawyers and clients alike) respond better to olive branches than thorns.

Ultimately, you will need to work closely with your attorney to reach a resolution and an end to the lawsuit. This may take time. Your opponent may be unwilling to practice nonjustice and may continue making unreasonable demands. To minimize your suffering, you should continue practicing nonjustice even if your opponent will not join you. You cannot control what other people do. If they want to continue inflicting suffering upon themselves, that is their business. But by remaining steadfast in your resolve not to seek justice yourself, you will restore your happiness immediately and speed the lawsuit toward conclusion.

Are you rewarding a justice-seeking plaintiff by acquiescing to their demands? No. The goal is always to resolve conflicts and restore *your* happiness as quickly as possible. By compromising, you are doing exactly that. Remember the following observation from chapter 14: "Most lawsuits end exactly the way a nonjustice request begins: by the plaintiff asking for help *and the defendant granting the request in some from of compromise.*" You demonstrate the error of seeking justice by remaining peaceful and compromising despite being attacked, not by prolonging the dispute when it is in your power to end it—or, worse, by seeking justice yourself. It is not your job to teach the plaintiff a lesson or prevent him from getting away with something. It is your job to be happy. Offering help to even an undeserving plaintiff can purchase much happiness indeed. So, ask yourself this: "What exactly is my happiness worth? Is it really worth being right?"

Does nonjustice apply to everyday life? Can it improve my relationships with my family, friends, teachers, co-workers, and employers?

Absolutely. Practicing nonjustice in all of your relationships can eliminate conflicts and help guarantee your peace and happiness. Although nonjustice may seem at first to be a legal concept, it is foremost a teaching for improving relationships between people. Whether you are having an argument with your children, a spat with your spouse, a battle with your parents, a disagreement with your teacher, a quarrel with your friend, a fight with your co-worker, or a war with your employer, nonjustice glows like a beacon in the darkness to show you the way out. No matter how large, small, or painful, there is no conflict that cannot be resolved by practicing nonjustice. I practice nonjustice in my own life, and my relationships with my children, wife, family members, friends, and business associates have become more calm and peaceful, allowing me to enjoy the people around me and them to enjoy me. My disputes with others do not last as long as they used to or become as intense, and I am able to avoid many conflicts altogether. Nonjustice really has changed my life for the better. I am a more happy person, and I am more successful as well. Conflicts and negativity that have so often distracted me from achieving my goals are now quickly overcome and eliminated.

Everything *you* need to be a more happy and successful person is right here too. You now know that seeking justice when you are wronged is the cause of your suffering, not the answer. You now know that the trial of the people who hurt you is the most important trial of your life because during this trial you must choose between getting justice and experiencing happiness. You now know that getting justice is an addiction that can destroy you. You now know how to overcome this addiction by practicing nonjustice. And you now have access to an always-open court of Divine creation to help you practice nonjustice and win the most important trial of your life. If you want your difficult relationships to improve, *right now*, you need only turn to chapter 11 and submit your grievances to The Nonjustice System for resolution. You cannot control what others do and feel, but you can take control of your own happiness. By doing so, you increase the happiness of everyone around you.

Acknowledgments

With humble gratitude to Sumi C. Chong, Esq., William Perkins, and Martin D. Kimmel, A.I.A., for their wisdom and inspiration as truly enlightened spiritual friends and guides. In the same vein to the members and attenders of the Kennett Monthly Meeting of the Religious Society of Friends. With deep reverence for my editors, occasional critics, and steadfast champions: Christine S. Kimmel, Esq., whose skills as a lawyer and a writer are exceeded only by her intuitive spirituality, love, loyalty, and patience as a wife, companion, and mother; and Stephen L. Everhart, who sets high the bar as a person and a writer, driving me always to reach beyond my grasp. All remaining errors in the text are mine alone. Finally, with many thanks to Larry J. Nulton, Ph.D., who provided me with steady support, encouragement, and an early laboratory to experiment with the teachings in this book.

—James P. Kimmel, Jr., J.D.

About the Author

James P. Kimmel, Jr., J.D. holds a doctorate in jurisprudence from the University of Pennsylvania. He served an internship with the Philadelphia District Attorney's office, a judicial clerkship with a United States federal trial court judge, and practiced law with two of the most prominent law firms in the United States. Attorney Kimmel has appeared before courts across the nation on behalf of a wide variety of clients, from indigent families seeking food stamps and prisoners seeking better conditions of confinement to some of the wealthiest individuals and largest corporations in the world. Recognized as an expert in written advocacy and legal analysis, Attorney Kimmel has been retained as a consultant by law firms around the country to assist them in developing legal strategies and drafting legal arguments. He also holds a United States patent as the inventor of the first automated legal research assignment and ordering system. Attorney Kimmel is the author of the novel *Nevaeh* (a semi-finalist for the 2003 University of Tennessee Press/Peter Taylor Prize for the Novel); the short story *The Tokamak* (a semi-finalist for the 2003 William Faulkner Creative Writing Award); and the illustrated children's book *The Old Architect.*

In addition to writing, speaking, and teaching about the principles of nonjustice, Attorney Kimmel maintains a private law practice in the suburbs of Philadelphia that focuses upon the practice of nonjustice law. Attorney Kimmel is also the president and founder of the Nonjustice Foundation (www.nonjustice.org). He lives in the country with his wife and two children. For more information, please visit www.AttorneyKimmel.com.

For More Information

Learn more about nonjustice and how it can be used to transform your life and the world by visiting the Nonjustice Foundation at **www.nonjustice.org.**

About the Cover

The symbol of nonjustice is the scales of justice with the chains holding the weight pans cut free, converting them into the Scales of Nonjustice. The Scales of Nonjustice always hang in perfect balance whenever we cease weighing each other's wrongs. By severing the chains of justice, we free ourselves and the world.

Hampton Roads Publishing Company

. . . for the evolving human spirit

HAMPTON ROADS PUBLISHING COMPANY publishes books on a variety of subjects, including metaphysics, spirituality, health, visionary fiction, and other related topics.

We also create on-line courses and sponsor an *Applied Learning Series* of author workshops. For a current list of what is available, go to www.hrpub.com, or request the ALS workshop catalog at our toll-free number.

For a copy of our latest trade catalog, call toll-free, 800-766-8009, or send your name and address to:

HAMPTON ROADS PUBLISHING COMPANY, INC.
1125 STONEY RIDGE ROAD • CHARLOTTESVILLE, VA 22902
e-mail: hrpc@hrpub.com • www.hrpub.com